LEGION

A Texan's Adventure in the French Foreign Legion

Richard Trevino, Jr.

ISBN 978-1-0980-1022-5 (paperback)
ISBN 978-1-0980-1023-2 (digital)

Christian Faith Publishing, Inc.
832 Park Avenue
Meadville, PA 16335
www.christianfaithpublishing.com

Printed in the United States of America

To my mother,
I love you.

Chapter 1

My name is Richard Trevino Jr., and I was born in a small South Texas town called Alice located in Jim Wells County. My parents are Richard and Celia (Sally) Trevino, and they were married about six months before I was born—my father was eighteen, and my mother was nineteen. Back then, it wasn't very popular to have a child out of wedlock, it was one of those things that was looked down upon in the Mexican-American community. So my parents got married, and they loved each other very much, and I think they would have gotten married with each other regardless if Mom was pregnant or not.

Alice, in 1971, didn't have many jobs to offer a young family, you either worked as a ranch hand or worked in the oil fields, and if you were lucky enough to find a job with the city or county, you really had it made. My father worked on ranches all his life, and that's what he loved to do. Still to this day, when you enter into his house, you can hear the galloping of horses and cowboys firing their six shooters blaring from the television coming from one of his favorite black and white Westerns. I guess that's the old vaquero in him. After about a year of bouncing around different ranches, and after Mom complained enough, we moved to San Marcos. Mom's side of the family is originally from San Marcos, so naturally, Mom wanted to be closer to her family; she missed them a lot.

In the Mexican-American community, the mothers and grand-mothers are the nucleus of the family household. They are the ones who take care of you when you are sick, feed you when you're hungry, hold you when you're sad, and discipline you when needed, and when we were looking for wisdom and guidance, we always turned to them. When you're young, you never imagine what life would be like without them, it never crossed my mind. I guess that was another reason why we moved to San Marcos, it must've crossed my mother's mind. She missed and loved her mother very much.

San Marcos is a small college town located just south of Austin and north of San Antonio located on Interstate Highway 35. Back in the '70s, there were only three things that brought you to this town, Southwest Texas State University, Aquarena Springs Amusement Park, and third, and best reason even to this day, is the San Marcos River—where we found ourselves swimming and picnicking from its banks every summer on the weekends. Back then, there were no big outlet malls or large car dealerships running up and down IH 35. San Marcos was a small and quiet town.

Between 1972 and 1979, my father had bounced around a lot of different jobs, and at the same, time we bounced around a lot of different homes never really being stable. Within that time period, we had moved at least five times. I remember my father working in all these different jobs that had nothing in common with each other—he worked in road construction, cotton mills, and restaurants, and I even remember a slaughterhouse. He never lasted longer than a few months to a few years at each job, he just wasn't happy, I guess. During this hectic time, my brother was born (John Paul), it was 1978, and I was seven years old. I remember being so happy that I was finally a big brother, I finally had someone to play with. That feeling was short-lived since he was a pain in the butt! Yeah, if he wasn't pooping something out, he was burping something up, too much for a seven-year-old kid to handle, but I still loved him, he was my little brother, so I got used to it.

It was now 1979, and my father had learned about a job in Wimberley working as a ranch hand from a friend of his. Wimberley is a small-town, west of San Marcos, located on the edge of the hill country. He interviewed with the foreman and was hired on the spot. Within a week, we packed all our belongings and moved to the Fulton Ranch. It was like the Beverly Hillbillies but in reverse. I was eight years old when this sudden change in our lifestyle occurred, living out in the country was something new to us. The ranch house that we moved into was built in the late 1800s or early 1900s and looked every bit of its age.

We were the only family on this four-thousand-acre ranch, besides the foreman and his wife. His children had long since married and moved on. Having moved from a neighborhood with friends and people all around at any given time to an old ranch house in the middle of nowhere, with no one around for miles, this was my first culture shock to experience. It's hard going from having friends to play with to absolutely no one within a week. Me and my little brother were the only kids on that ranch.

I had to start working as a ranch hand, feeding horses and cattle, to help my father. During the summers, I would go with my father twice a day, once in the morning and once in the afternoon. During the school year, I only went once in the afternoon. Feeding the horses was hard. In the hot summer months, we started feeding the animals at six in the morning. We started by loading around 30 buckets full of grain—weighing between 30 and 40 pounds each, depending on how much grain you put in it. I remember having to carry those buckets to the feeding troughs, sometimes two at a time, and lifting the buckets up to my chest and pouring them into the troughs. When you're eight years old and scrawny, 40 pounds is a lot of weight to handle, but I got used to it. We would have to refill the buckets at least five times to feed all 150 horses, plus hay. We would be finished between nine thirty and ten thirty in the morning.

After feeding the horses, we would return to the old ranch house. The roads weren't paved, so everywhere you went, you were a dusty mess afterwards. My father dropped me off at home, and he would return to work to finish the rest of his duties, mending fences, moving horses and cattle, and also checking the property for trespassers. Before leaving the house, my father always kissed my mother on the cheek and told her that he loved her. With work and my chores out of the way, I had a few hours before I had to return to work in the afternoon, which gave me just enough time to go down to the river for a swim. The Blanco River cut through the Fulton Ranch and was within walking distance of the old house. There was a lot to do on the ranch, but my favorite was to swim. On our part of the river, it was extremely shallow. In some areas, the water eroded small pools into the limestone river bottom, which made natural swimming pools

I remember running out the back door of the old ranch house, yelling to my mother, "I'm going down to the river I'll be back later!" I can still hear my little brother's feet, smacking on the hardwood floors, chasing me out the door trying to follow me, saying, "I'm going too!" Turning around and scooping him up in my arms, and saying, "Oh no, you're not!"

He would squirm and kick in my arms, trying to break free asking with his saddest face, "Why not?"

Then I would tell him, "Because you're too small and barefoot, and plus your diapers keep falling!"

Running to the front of the house, with him in my arms, trying to catch my father before he backed out of the driveway, "Dad, he's trying to follow me again."

My father would ask my little brother, "Want to go with me instead and check for trespassers?"

My brother would return with a quick, "Hell yeah!" And off they would go.

I remember many times taking a shortcut and running through the house to get to the backyard to a trail that led down to the river. Darting past my mother, she would ask me in her soft Spanish accent, "Mijo (pronounced mee-ho) you're not going to give me a hug and kiss goodbye before you leave?" Halfway out of the house, I would have to double back, "Sorry, Mom," and give her a hug. She would then always tell me, "Watch out for rattlesnakes and water moccasins, and don't lift or move any rocks!"

As I was running out the back door, I would say, "Okay, Mom!"

I had a dog named Shorty who would follow me down to the river. He was a funny-looking mutt with the markings of a Doberman Pincher but was only a foot tall at the shoulders, you know how the old saying goes, beggars can't be choosers. He was the only friend that I had out there. We would run straight down to the river and stay in the water the rest of the day, I felt like the luckiest kid in the world.

I didn't have a watch, but I always knew when lunch or dinner was ready. It was when you could smell the tortillas Mom was making that were being carried down to the river on a lite breeze from the ranch house. "Come on, Shorty, lunch is ready!" We would run back home as fast as we could to eat and head back to the river before having to return to work feeding the horses that afternoon, following the same procedure as in the morning. This went on for eight years uninterrupted until the ranch was sold, and we had to move out. The time that we spent on that ranch was the most fun I had in my life, even though it was labor intensive and the poorest time of our lives, I wouldn't change it for the world.

After leaving the ranch, we moved to the other side of Wimberley a few miles from the junction where Ranch Road 12 and Highway 32 meet. My father was tossed back into the grind of trying to find a job and trying to support our family. It was a very hectic and trying time for the entire family. Mom always supported my father and our family; she was our foundation. When times were tough, Mom always went out of her way to make us happy and make us feel good about ourselves. There was never any doubt in her eyes that we wouldn't make it through this rough period or any rough period that life would throw our way. With her strength and her love, I understood why sometimes we didn't get gifts for Christmas or birthdays. The only thing that mattered was that we were together. My father was having trouble finding steady work in Wimberley, and after a couple of years of this, my parents decided to move the family back to San Marcos.

On moving back to San Marcos, our parents enrolled us in school. I was a sophomore in high school, and my little brother was in the second grade. It was another culture shock for me moving back into town. There were people everywhere and cars all over the place, driving at all hours of the night. I was having trouble sleeping and having to lock your doors and chaining up your bike had to be learned quickly. I wasn't used to any of this, but I soon adapted to this new lifestyle as I did when we moved out into the country. My high school years were uneventful. I wasn't into sports or part of any types of clubs. I was that dorky kid that didn't have any luck with my grades or the girls. All I wanted to do was to graduate and get out of high school and San Marcos.

My mother's father was in the Army and fought in Europe during World War II, and her brother was also in the Army and served in Vietnam. They would tell me stories of their time in the military and their tours overseas. Their stories always sounded so exciting to me, and I wanted to see foreign lands and experience the same adventures they talked about. So, between my junior and senior years of high school in 1987, I joined the Texas National Guard and completed basic training that summer at Fort Benning, Georgia. I returned home to finish my senior year, and the following summer, I went back to Fort Benning to complete my advance individual training as an infantry soldier. After completing my training in June 1989, I returned home to enjoy the rest of the summer and try to figure out my next move. It took me an entire year to figure out that I wasn't going anywhere. At the end of the summer of 1990, I joined the regular Army, and I was shipped off to Fort Lewis, Washington, and attached to the 9th Infantry Division.

A few months after arriving at Fort Lewis, Iraq invaded Kuwait and was threatening to invade Saudi Arabia. In response, the United States started building a coalition force in Saudi Arabia to defend against an Iraqi invasion. The mission was called Desert Shield. In Ft Lewis at the time, the Army was asking for volunteers from its infantry battalions for immediate deployment to Saudi Arabia. I volunteered, and within a week, I was shipped to Fort Bragg, North Carolina. I was attached to a radio team of about twenty men, and we were briefed on our mission and told that we wouldn't be assigned to an American unit but to a Saudi Arabian Division. Our mission was to be the communications link between US and Saudi Arabian forces. We landed in Riyadh, Saudi Arabia, in mid-November and spent Thanksgiving there. The USO had a show for us, and Bob Hope performed.

In mid-December, we left for the desert in a convoy of about ten trucks, a mixture of Humvees and deuce and a half trucks, to search for the Saudi Arabian Division near the Kuwaiti border. While driving in the empty desert, I couldn't help but think back to just six months earlier, I was floating down the San Marcos River in tubes and enjoying the summer with my friends. Now here I am, in full battle gear, heading out into the desert, looking for a Saudi Arabian Division. To make matters worse, I didn't speak any Arabic. I couldn't even say please or thank you.

We were given small booklets when we arrived in country to teach us the Arab language and customs, but it didn't work. The search lasted the entire day, rolling over sand dunes at times and feeling completely lost. I was nineteen and scared, and I had never seen a country like this before. Just six months earlier, it was my first time out of Texas, besides basic training. We found the Saudi division late in the evening and slept in our trucks. The next morning, we found a Marine and Special Forces radio team in place, and they gave us the SITREP (situational report) on what was going on in the Saudi camp and troop movement along the border. Our radio team adapted quickly, and we learned a little of the Arab language and customs while attached to the Saudi forces.

Being a part of a radio team, we had satellite communication with General Schwarzkopf's command and the United States. We weren't allowed to use the satellite communications for personal use. Early one morning, while on guard duty, I snuck into our TOC (Tactical Operations Center) and used the satellite phone and called home. My mother answered the phone, and she was very happy to hear from me. I explained I didn't have long to talk on the phone, so she passed the phone to my father, little brother, and my grandfather. The phone was returned to my mother, and I asked her to put my grandmother on the line, who was diagnosed with diabetes at the time and lost her foot to the disease. My mother told me that she was traveling around Texas with one of her sister's visiting relatives for the holidays, seeing how she wasn't able to do so the year before due to her illness and money problems. I told my mother to tell her, when she gets back, that I love her, and that I would send her a letter every week and not to worry about me.

In January, the bombing of Iraq started, and the mission designation changed from Operation Desert Shield to Operation Desert Storm. During the air campaign, the Iraqi forces tried to lure the coalition forces into a ground battle by attacking the border town of Khafji, along the Saudi Arabian and the Kuwaiti border. It didn't work, and they were beaten back by US forces. Our camp was about fifteen miles southwest of Khafji, and a few days later, the Saudi Division—we were with—moved into the city to give the US forces more support.

We knew our ground offensive was coming soon, but we didn't know when. While in Khafji, I snuck back into the TOC to make one last call before our ground offensive was launched. One last chance to say goodbye, one last chance to say I love you to my family, not knowing if I was going to be dead or alive in the coming weeks. Just hearing the voice of someone you love puts a person at ease. I asked to speak with my grandmother again but was told she was still traveling around the state, visiting family and that she wouldn't be back anytime soon. I asked my mother again to tell her I loved her and to reassure her I would be home soon.

It was a good thing that I had slipped back into the TOC when I did because the very next day, we were briefed on the ground offensive. The plan was to first push into Kuwait by highway, through the city of Khafji. The reason they wanted us to use the highway was to bypass the minefields and obstacles, maneuver our vehicles out into the desert in a horizontal formation after crossing the border, and move across the southern part of Kuwait. Our division had three major objectives it had to secure, each objective was estimated to take two to three weeks to secure. Our first objective was securing a highway overpass, the second objective was a school, and the third objective was a Kuwaiti television station that was being used as the main Iraqi headquarters in the city of Kuwait.

This objective, we were told, was going to be the hardest objective to secure due to the Iraqi Republican Guard; they intended to defend their headquarters to the last man. After the briefing, we prepared our gear and loaded the vehicles to move out the next morning. I couldn't get any rest that evening as the idea of going into battle kept playing in my head. I kept wondering if I was going to be alive by the following afternoon. The explosions didn't help me get any rest either. The Navy had a battleship in the Gulf, and it was firing its big guns all along the border. Air Force aircrafts were flying bombing missions near Khafji. The buildings shook with every explosion, shattering windows and nocking plaster off the ceilings and walls—those guys got pretty close.

We moved out before dawn the next day, and I was the driver of a Humvee soft shell pick-up with three other people including an officer. The Saudi and Arabic coalition forces took the lead, and we fell in behind. We were the last group of vehicles in a convoy that stretched for miles. We got on the highway headed north into Kuwait at full speed. After crossing the border, I noticed something was wrong. We stayed on the highway, never getting off, and we passed the area where we were supposed to enter the desert. Instead, we stayed on the highway and stopped periodically when the Saudi forces stopped. Smoke and explosions were everywhere, and there was so much talk on the radios that it was very confusing, it seemed like no one knew what was going on.

Off in the distance ahead of the convoy, US planes were taking out ground targets. It was an incredible and very welcoming sight to see that the Air Force was covering our advance. We stayed on the highway and started getting closer to Kuwait City. By that afternoon, we had almost reached our third objective. We had moved so fast that we had to double back and find the second objective, which was the school, and set up a temporary TOC.

While securing the school, we met Kuwaiti resistance fighters, and they told us that the Iraqis were leaving Kuwait City and headed north back to Iraq in a large convoy of trucks and tanks. As they were telling us this, US planes were destroying the very convoy on the "highway of death." We moved out the next morning and headed for the third and final objective without any incident. The Iraqis had retreated across the border to the north leaving a mass of equipment, weapons, and personal items behind. It seemed as though they left in such a hurry that they only took the shirts on their backs with them.

A few weeks later, the peace treaty was signed, the war was over, and the entire country erupted in celebration. After the peace treaty was signed, I had snuck back into our TOC and called home to give everyone the good news. I talked to my father, brother, and my grandfather. I told my mother, "Mom, we won the war, I'll be coming home soon!"

"That's good, mijo, when you get home, we'll have a big party for you," she said.

I then asked her, "Let me speak to Grandma, I want to tell her the good news that we won the war!"

My mother paused and said to me, "Mijo, uh," she paused again, "Mijo, Grandma passed away four months ago."

I choked out. "What?"

My mother explained, "We didn't want you to go to war with her death on your mind."

I couldn't believe what I was hearing. I was crushed. My celebration turned to sorrow in an instant. I wrote her a letter every week the entire time thinking she was alive. I couldn't say anything, I couldn't think I just said bye and hung up the phone. I was upset at first, but after a few tears and some thinking, I understood why they kept her death from me. I understood they wanted me to concentrate all my emotions on the war and not worry about her death, they wanted me home alive and not in a box. It was a tough decision to make, but I respect the decision that was made as a family to protect me.

Chapter 2

The war was over, and in a few months, I was back in the states. I was sent back to Fort Lewis, Washington, where I stayed there for a year until I received orders for Korea to serve with the 2nd Infantry Division for a one year tour of duty. I arrived in April of 1992 and was assigned to the 1st of the 506th Infantry Battalion, "CURR-AHEE," at Camp Greaves located at the DMZ.

While in Korea, I read a book called "Mouthful of Rocks," it was about one man's experience in the French Foreign Legion, and it sparked my interest. I wanted to learn more about the Legion. So, on one of my weekend passes, I traveled to Seoul, visited the French Embassy, and picked up an information packet on the Legion. In the packet, there was a sheet of paper that had a listing of addresses and phone numbers of recruiting stations in France. There was also a booklet that had information on the Legion's history and their modern-day missions. I read it from front to back on the bus ride back to camp. For now, I put the Legion in the back of my mind for the time being and concentrated on the rest of my tour in Korea.

This was one of the toughest places I had ever been, up to this point, as an infantry soldier, you walked everywhere, and the terrain was unforgiving. The country felt like it was made entirely of hills and mountain ranges. Once you crested one hill, there was another one waiting for you on the other side it seemed endless. I could never imagine having to fight a war in this type of terrain. I don't know how those guys, during the Korean War, survived the weather and terrain plus fighting for every hill between Seoul and the southern border of China. It was a true test of their strength, will, and determination, which is truly amazing to me. I have a lot of respect for the soldiers that served in the Korean War, for they were in hell on earth. It saddens me that it's called the "Forgotten War." I wish it was recognized more often out of respect for the soldiers who sacrificed their lives for freedom.

My tour was finally over in April 1993, and I was reassigned to the 101st Airborne Division at Fort Campbell in Kentucky and finished my last year in the Army there, and boy was I ready for the civilian life. I was honorably discharged in May of 1994 and went home to start my new life as a civilian, no more deployments, no more weapons or equipment to be cleaned, and no more inspections. I could finally get on with my life. As soon as I arrived in Texas, I found a good job working for a cement factory and living in Austin. I was on my way to becoming that civilian I wanted to be, or so I thought, something was wrong deep inside. I was having problems adjusting to this new life.

Coming from a very structured, disciplined, and rigid lifestyle, and going to a lifestyle that had no structure or discipline was a very strange experience for me. I felt like the people around me, coworkers, family, and friends didn't understand me; and I was having problems understanding them. I didn't have anyone to relate too. I felt alone and isolated, so naturally, I turned to the bottle as a friend, started drinking heavily, got into a lot of bar room fights, and lost touch with reality. I quit my job at the cement factory and bounced around several different jobs for the next couple of years, but never really being content always feeling misunderstood. I wasn't living the terrific civilian life that I thought I was going to be living after the military. I had moved several times in that two-year time period settling back down in San Marcos.

On the move back to San Marcos, I had found one of my old duffel bags, in my father's storage shed, that I hadn't seen since leaving the Army and decided to dig through it to relive some old memories. In doing so, I came across the information packet about the Legion that I had picked up from the French Embassy while in Korea. I read the information packet again, and it really sparked my interest in the Legion. I decided that this would be a strong consideration for the next move in my life. I felt that the civilian life was undisciplined, and I needed that discipline back in my life, but I didn't want to join the American army again. I wanted a new adventure, and I wanted to experience the world through different eyes and not through American eyes. After a couple of months thinking and pondering of what I was getting myself into, I finally built up enough courage to dial one of the numbers on the information packet, which was to a recruiting station located in Paris. After dialing the number, I held the phone up to my ear not expecting anything to happen.

It scared the crap out of me when the phone started ringing on the other end of the line, and I almost dropped the phone and said out loud, "Damn, number actually works!"

Someone on the other end answered in French, "Legion Etrangere Recruitment."

I then asked, "I need some information on the Legion?"

The person replied with a strong Eastern Bloc accent, "Oh, English, wait!"

A few minutes later, another legionnaire came on the line who spoke English with a German accent and explained that I needed to fly into Charles de Gaulle International Airport in Paris, take a train to the heart of the city, find a taxi to hand him the address that was on the information packet, and he would drop me off at the front gates. Sounds easy enough, I thought, now all I have to do was explain my plans to my family and convince them that I wasn't crazy. They immediately thought I was out of my mind. I explained to them how I was feeling and how I needed this to feel like I fit in somewhere again.

My family was upset with my decision to leave again, but they knew I really wanted to do this and realized that I needed a drastic change in my life to get out of this rut I was in. So, I bought my tickets, and when the time came, my parents took me to the airport in Houston toward the end of December in 1995. When my parents dropped me off our goodbyes were cold, they were upset that I was leaving again. As the car drove off, I could see my mother crying in the front seat through the window. It was hard for me seeing her go like that and it was understandable why they were upset I had only been out of the Army for two years and here I was leaving again, no telling for how long this time, joining the French army.

The flight to France was long, and normally it was easy for me to fall asleep on flights, but what made this one so long was that I kept thinking about my family and especially my mother crying as they drove away in the car. I felt so bad for putting her through this because I didn't know for sure if I was ever going to see her again. The plane landed at Charles de Gaulle International Airport, thank god it was in the middle of the day. I walked out of the plane, into the terminal, and thought to myself, What the hell have I gotten myself into? I couldn't read anything, the only thing I read was the word, "train," marked on arrows, which I followed and eventually led me to a ticket booth where I bought a ticket to Paris. The train was full of people from different cultures and ethnicities, and I couldn't understand a single word anyone was saying. I never felt so alone like that before in my life. It was another culture shock that I would have to adapt too. I should have been used to these types of changes in my life by now, but I guess it's something you never get used too.

We arrived in the city, and I exited the subway station around two in the afternoon somewhere in Paris, I can't even remember where. I was starting to get hungry, so I wandered around the streets looking for somewhere to eat. By this time, I only had $60 left in my pocket. I found a small hole in the wall café and sat down on one of the tables outside. After a few minutes, a waiter came out and gave me a menu and a glass of water.

He asked me something in French, and I shrugged my shoulders and pointed at the menu. He soon realized that I didn't speak French and took the menu from my hands then motioned for me to stay seated with his hands. A short time later, he arrived with a sandwich and an Orangina. I shrugged my shoulders again and showed him the money I had, and he quickly snatched $15 out of my hands and said, "Merci!" He turned around with a grin and walked back into the café, and I never saw him again. At the time, I felt like I got ripped off, and boy was I pissed, but I couldn't even argue my point because I didn't speak the language, so I had to swallow my pride, and let it slide. After that, I was down to $45, and I still needed to find a taxi. From the café, I could see the top of the Eiffel Tower poking itself above the buildings down the street. After eating, I walked toward where I thought the Eiffel Tower should be. About an hour later, after winding in and out of streets and crossing a river, I found the Eiffel Tower and stayed there for about thirty minutes just looking at this amazing structure that I had only seen pictures of in school books.

Soon after, I flagged a taxi down and gave him the address to the Legion recruiting station, and then I showed him how much money I had. He shook his head, barked something in French at me, turned around, switched the meter on, and then took off with enough force that it pushed me into the back seat. He drove me across town into the suburbs of Paris on a ride, which felt like it lasted forever, but in reality, it only lasted around twenty minutes. I couldn't wait to get out of the taxi, I thought I was going to die.

We stopped in the middle of a street somewhere in the suburbs, and he looked in the rearview mirror and angrily said something in French. He then pointed to the meter, and it showed an outrageous amount of money in French francs. I was staring at the meter wide-eyed. I couldn't believe the amount that was being shown. I then showed him how much money I had, and he quickly snatched all of it out of my hands. Now I was completely broke. He then pointed to a building that said GENDARME (police station) and yelled at me, "Legion!"

I exited the taxi and was about to close the door when he sped off, and the door closed by itself leaving me standing in the middle of the street in a cloud of exhaust smoke. I walked into the station, expecting this to be the Legion recruiting station and said, "French Foreign Legion?"

A man sitting behind a desk, in a police officer's uniform, squinted his eyes and twisted his head. He didn't understand what I was saying, so I showed him the address, and he nodded his head and walked me outside into the street. He started pointing and waving his left hand up and down the street and giving me directions in French. I didn't understand a single word he said, but I acted like I did, nodded my head, and said thank you in English. I walked off in the direction he pointed.

I had walked for a couple of hours looking for the recruiting station. It was starting to get dark now, I didn't know if I was going in the right direction. I thought that I was lost until I came across what looked like an ancient fortified berm, which had two large wooden doors with a sign that read "Legion Etrangere" (Foreign Legion). I knocked on the door, and a short Filipino guy, dressed in an olive drab combat uniform with a web belt and a white kepi on his head, opened the door and asked me something in French. I told him in English that I was looking for the French Foreign Legion recruiting station, and to my surprise he responded with, "You've come to the right place." He led me into a side room next to the front gates and asked me to dump everything that was in my bag on a table that was in the middle of the room.

I told him I didn't have anything, just personal belongings. He said he didn't care, he needed to make sure that I didn't have any drugs or weapons. After looking through my stuff, he told me to take off my clothes and patted me down. He then told me to put my clothes back on, led me to the barracks, issued me a green jogging suit, and said that I needed to wear this while on this post. I changed, and afterward, he took me in to an office where there was a legionnaire sitting at a desk with a typewriter in front of him. The person asked me to sit down in English with a strong German accent. I recognize that voice. It was the same guy on the phone who I spoke to back in the states a few months before.

He said he needed to get some information from me and asked where I was from and why I wanted to join the Legion. He also took my height and weight. When we were finished, he took me up to the third floor of the barracks where there were fifteen other recruits already in the process of cleaning the barracks from top to bottom. We walked into one of the rooms, and he showed me my bunk and told me that we would be marched to breakfast at five in the morning. I just missed dinner and had to help the other recruits clean the barracks.

I walked into the restroom, where there were some recruits cleaning, and asked if they needed any help. All I got back in response was blank stares from the group, and again nobody spoke any English. These guys were from the Eastern Bloc countries like Czechoslovakia, Poland, and Russia—from the old Soviet Union. We were a sorry group of rejects and misfits all looking for a new life in the Legion. We cleaned for about half an hour, and I started to get hungry. The sandwich that I had eaten earlier was completely burned off by the walk and the cleaning. I was starving, and we couldn't leave the building to get anything to eat or make any phone calls. By this time, it was around nine o'clock at night, so I snuck back to my bunk to lie down and get some rest. While lying there, I thought to myself, What the hell did I get my crazy ass into this time? I then slowly drifted off to sleep.

The next morning, at five o'clock, which was Sunday, we were marched to breakfast. On the way to the chow hall, I was trying to figure out what I wanted for breakfast, scrambled eggs with bacon? No, an omelet with mushrooms, onions and green peppers, yeah, an omelet, that's what I'm going to have—it's a lot bigger, and I'm really hungry again. We entered the chow hall and walked past the serving counter. There was nothing there—no server, no eggs, no bacon frying, and no omelet. I asked myself, What the hell is going on here? Everyone walked toward a cart filled with baguettes (French bread), ripping a piece off, then going to a counter and collecting a packet of butter, a packet of jelly, and a large cup of coffee then sitting down to eat breakfast. Is this all that we're having for breakfast a piece of bread? I thought. Well, it is Sunday, maybe French cooks don't work on Sunday mornings or something?

After breakfast, they lined us up outside in front of the chow hall, and the legionnaire chose me and four other recruits to stay and work in the chow hall for the rest of the day. Cool, I was still hungry, and I can steal some more bread. The day passed without any incident, and we worked through lunch and dinner. We were able to eat as much as we wanted, more like as much as we could steal without getting caught. We finished around eight that evening, and we were marched back to the barracks with full stomachs. Upon arriving back to the barracks, we were informed that we would be going to the main recruiting station, which was in the South of France in a town called Aubagne, by train the next morning.

The next morning, we turned in our jogging suits, and were allowed to put our civilian clothes back on. We were rushed through breakfast, which was the same damn thing as the morning before—a piece of bread, butter, jelly, and a cup of coffee. What the hell is going on here? I asked myself, but before I could give it any more thought, we were ordered to get outside and get into a military truck, which took us to a train station where we boarded a train, which took us to Aubagne. Aubagne is where the main recruiting station is located and home to the 1st Regiment Etranger.

At Aubagne, we were reissued the green jogging suits, and for the next couple of weeks, we were given mental exams, physical exams, fitness tests, aptitude tests, and a background check through Interpol; and our passports were confiscated. In one of the interviews, I was asked if I wanted to change my identity. I said, "No, I wanted to keep my family name." I had nothing to hide, and I wasn't running away from anything. The exams and tests lasted for two weeks. Toward the end of the second week, we finally found out who was accepted into the Legion. Out of the 16 recruits that came from Paris, I was the only one that was accepted into the Legion. There were a total of forty who came from different recruiting stations from all over France, who were finally accepted into the Legion. They took our green jogging suits and issued us brand-new military gear, which included our battle dress uniform, boots, and a green beret with a gold pin, which had a symbol of a grenade with flames shooting out of the top of it. We also all had our hair buzzed off.

Chapter 3

We were finally assembled and shipped by train to a town called Castelnaudary, where the 4th Regiment Etranger is located, which is the training regiment of the Legion. By this time, it was the beginning of January and extremely cold, but we arrived at the regiment with a warm welcome of screaming and yelling and calisthenics to shock us and to also show us who was in charge. I was still having problems understanding the French language, but I was catching on pretty quick. What was helping me out was the fact that I spoke two languages—English and Spanish—and French has a combination of both English and Spanish words in it, so I was catching on faster than the other recruits who only spoke one language. The recruits, who were having the most problems, were the ones who had to learn a completely different alphabet like the Chinese and Russian recruits who got punched in the stomach a lot for their problems with the language.

We were assigned to one of the training companies and got issued more gear and immediately sent to the farm. The farm is a training site that is in the surrounding countryside of Castelnaudary. There are three training companies, and each one has a farm of its own to maintain. On each property, there is one large two-story farmhouse and a large barn. Here, we were trained in patrolling, raids, physical fitness, and the French language mixed in with a lot of hazing and starvation. Starvation is one of the fundamentals of the Legion you can't escape, it's instilled in you early on in your training because there will be times when resupply is out of the question, and you have to survive off of whatever your surroundings—urban or in the wild. They teach you to barter and steal—if necessary.

I remember being so hungry at times that we would dig through the trash cans in the back of the farmhouse looking for food like animals. They would feed us as little as possible and trained us to exhaustion. For example, in the mornings, they fed us a piece of bread and coffee, lunch was a piece of sausage and a scoop of beans, and dinner was a bowl of soup. The instructors ate on a table that was elevated above ours and would heap their plates full of food and eat in front of us. The lower ranking instructors prepared the food for the recruits during the day and guarded the kitchen at night to ensure no one stole any food. After every meal, we cleaned all our dishes, pots, and pans in a water trough for farm animals behind the old farmhouse using rocks and gravel to scrub them clean.

There was no hot running water at the farm, so every shower was brutally cold. We didn't have any washer or dryers and had to wash our clothes by hand, in large sinks in the restrooms, which we also used to do personal hygiene. We would then hang them outside, hoping they would dry in the winter sun. This lasted for three weeks, I had left the states in mid-December, and now it was toward the end of January. I spent my twenty-fifth birthday at the farm. I can honestly say this was one of my worst birthdays ever.

At the end of the grueling three-week initiation course, we had a three-day forced march exercise that tested everything we had learned at the farm. In the Legion, the forced march is looked upon as both tradition and necessity, which goes back to the time before World War II when soldiers walked into battle and weren't trucked in or choppered in like today. In the Legion, marching long distances is a way to keep in touch with the early legionnaires. The Legion thrives off suffering and heartache. The forced march is a very effective training tool, but on the modern-day battlefield, it's not very tactical due to the Legion being a fast reaction force.

We would march all night, get tested during the day, rest for a few hours in the afternoon, and repeat the process the next evening. On the last night, we were completely exhausted and excited that the farm was finally going to be over. This was to be the longest and the hardest of the marches, which was between forty-five to fifty kilometers long (twenty-five to thirty miles). The next morning, at daybreak, we arrived at another farm where we had a small ceremony and where a commanding officer reminded us that we are taking an oath of honor and loyalty to the Legion. After singing "Le Boudin," we were able to don the coveted white kepi for the first time. I was pleased that we were leaving the farm, but we still had three months left of basic training, and we were far from done.

The next three months were filled with weapons training, hand-to-hand combat, forced marches, and a lot of French lessons. We even had drivers' training to receive our driver's license. While at Castelnaudary, I met a fellow American who was in another training company and was a week out from graduating basic training and about to leave for Aubagne, where everyone goes to receive their orders for their next duty assignment. I haven't contacted my family since leaving the states in December, and it was now the end of March. I was really worried about them, and I can only imagine what they were going through not knowing what had happened to me.

No one is allowed to make phone calls during basic training until the last two weeks before you graduate, so I gave him my parents' phone number. I asked him to call my family to let them know that I had gotten accepted into the Legion, I was going through basic training, and that I would contact them as soon as I was allowed. He did me the favor, and the next time I saw him, he told me that my family was doing fine and that they send their love.

At this point, I had about two more months left in training. The rest of basic training passed without any incidents. The training was hard but not impossible. You do everything they tell you to do, don't complain, and always try to do it right the first time, so you don't have a drill instructor yelling in your ear, dishing out some sort of punishment in the form of calisthenics, or in some cases, when you really messed up, a punch to the stomach. The soldiers in the Legion are a strong, fearless, and genuine type of people. Don't get me wrong, there were some bad apples in the bunch, which made for a good combination for when you're in combat.

Basic training was finally over, and the last couple of weeks at Castelnaudary were spent cleaning the barracks, equipment, and weapons that we used in the training company, getting everything ready for the next round of recruits. Within these two weeks, we were allowed one phone call to let our loved ones, or whoever we wanted to know, that we had completed and survived Legion basic training. We purchased phone cards at the post-exchange and were told that we only had five minutes each to contact someone. When it was my turn, I walked up to the phone, and I was completely nervous not knowing if anyone was going to answer my call. Some of the recruits didn't contact anyone and had to give up the phone after five minutes.

I dialed my parent's number, and it started ringing. After a few rings, to my surprise, the phone picked up, and it was my mother, she yelled, "It's lil' Rich!" to my father. The greetings were joyful and tearful. My family was happy to hear my voice and to know that I was still alive after five months of not knowing what had happened to me. It felt good hearing their voices again, I didn't feel so alone anymore. I didn't want to get off the phone, but I knew the other recruits wanted to talk to their families too, so I reassured them that I would be contacting them in the coming weeks as soon as I found out where I was going to be stationed.

I said goodbye, with a lump in my throat, and hung up the phone. After Castelnaudary, we were shipped back to Aubagne to get our orders for our first duty station. When we received our orders, I called back home immediately to let them know that I was going to be stationed in East Africa in a small country called Djibouti. My mother asked if I was going to come home before I got shipped off. I had to break the sad news to her that a legionnaire is not allowed to take leave overseas for the first five years of their contract. I could hear her crying on the other end of the line, and I tried to comfort her by saying that the four and a half years would pass quickly and that she wouldn't even notice the time that I was gone. It didn't work, and she was heartbroken. I felt like I had let her down. I said goodbye, told her that I loved her, and that I would call home as soon as I arrived in Africa.

Within a week, I was on a military-chartered plane with other Legion soldiers headed for Djibouti. By this time, it was mid-May. The flight lasted around fifteen hours, and no one talked or said anything to each other. We all knew that this was going to be a crap assignment. The plane landed late in the afternoon, I can't even remember what day it was I was so fatigued. We waited in the plane for about thirty minutes before given the okay to exit. The rear doors located behind the wings were open for us. The plane was mixed with both soldiers and civilians. The civilians exited on the right side of the plane and the legionnaire's exited on the left. Upon exiting the plane, our group was hit with a gust of wind that burned our skin. We raised our hands to shield our faces from the pain and then someone yelled, "The engines are still on!" We all ran around the wing to escape the engines blast, but once again, we were met with another blast of burning hot wind. It wasn't the engine's exhaust that was causing the painful burning, but in fact, it was the wind that was skimming across the runway and slamming into the group. The heat was incredible, and we immediately started to perspire. I tried hiding my shock from the extreme heat, but I could see it on everyone else's face too. That was just a taste of things to come.

There were two Legion trucks waiting on the tarmac—one for us, and the other for our gear. In the group, there were six legionnaires—three new recruits, a corporal, and two sergeants. We were trucked to the Legion headquarters in Djibouti called Qaurtier Montclair, home of the 13th Demi-brigade of the French Foreign Legion. We arrived at the post, ate dinner, and were quickly quarantined to our barracks and were not allowed to leave or go anywhere that night. The next day, we had a meeting with a sergeant from the admin part of the brigade, telling us that we would in-process and acclimatize to the heat for the following ten days. After ten days, we received our assignments. Me, another recruit, and the corporal got assigned to the reconnaissance squadron that was located about fifty miles north of the capital located in a small village called We'a (pronounced way-yah).

The other three stayed at Qaurtier Montclair, lucky bastards! The next day, we were picked up by a truck, which was escorted by a Jeep sent from the squadron. The ride to the camp was a very hot and somber one. Poverty was everywhere, and the shantytowns lined the main highway, leading out of the city of Djibouti. The smell of raw sewage, mixed with the heat, was unbearable, and the stench was overwhelming. Every time we passed a shantytown, all the kids would gather near the road and throw rocks at our trucks. You could hear the thuds against the canvas covering the trucks. I guess that was our welcome! We finally arrived at the camp, which was enclosed by a chest high wall made of brick with a ten-foot high chain-link fence on it and was topped with concertina wire, which went all the way around the camp. For the next couple of days, we in-processed and were shown around the camp by a corporal.

There was a small post-exchange, an enlisted bar, NCO bar, an officer's bar, barracks, and a motor pool for the vehicles. I was assigned to first platoon, and after reporting to the platoon sergeant and the platoon's lieutenant, I was finally shown to the only phone on the post, which was located in a small booth in the headquarters building. I was allowed to call home and give my family my new address. It felt good knowing that I was going to be able to keep in touch with my family on a regular basis now after five months of complete silence.

The lieutenant, in the recon platoon I was assigned, had arrived a few weeks before me. He organized a field exercise in which he wanted to build cohesion and get to know the men in his platoon a lot better. The exercise took the entire platoon, in three deuce and a half trucks and a couple of Jeeps, north along the coast of Djibouti and camping near the Ethiopian border overlooking the Red Sea. The exercise helped us work as a team to survive off the land and sea. We had our regular military rations, supplies, and ammunition. Each day, we had two teams looking for food. One team would go out into the desert looking for animals to hunt, mainly gazelles. The other team would go out into the shoreline in rubber boats using spearguns, fishing rods, and whatever tools we could make to catch small sharks, fish, stingrays, and crabs. We ate everything we could catch. On one day, a group of four tribesmen, with camels and armed with AK-47s, came to our camp and bartered baskets of crab they had gathered in exchange for our military rations and supplies.

During this exercise, the lieutenant expressed to me that he wanted me to go to all the military schools, the Legion offered in

Djibouti, since I was the only English-speaking soldier in the platoon. It would really benefit the platoon that I had the military schools under my belt in case we had to work with American and British forces, they wanted to use me as a liaison.

About two months after the field exercise, the lieutenant signed me up for Jeep reconnaissance school. The 13th Demi-brigade conducts reconnaissance missions in several different ways. It utilizes a six-wheeled light armored tank called the ERC 90 Sagaies tank, the Renault 4x4 combat vehicle, which is about the same size and diameter of the US Army's old World War II era Jeep, mounted with a .50 caliber machine gun, on motorcycles, and on foot.

In the first week of the Jeep reconnaissance school, we learned operation, maintenance, and capabilities of the vehicle. The second week was on weapons, explosives (C4 shaped charges, antipersonnel mines and Bangalore torpedoes), camouflage, aircraft, and vehicle recognition—both enemy and friendly. The third week was spent out in the desert, learning movement techniques, land navigation, and incorporating everything we had learned from the weeks before. The training was always hard and tough, and they didn't bullshit around when it came to teaching you how to survive in combat. After completing the first school, I couldn't wait to start the next one. Immediately after the school, I reported to my lieutenant where he explained to me that the next school would be tank recon, followed by motorcycle recon, and a few months after, there would be a commando school. I was excited about all the schools that they were going to send me to. I felt really good about myself, I had started a new life, and everything was going exactly the way that I had planned.

A couple of months passed, and the next school was the tank school. We learned the general maintenance of the vehicle, driving the vehicle, and loading and firing its 90 mm cannon. The tank is a 6x6 armored vehicle that carries a crew of three and holds twenty cannon rounds and is mounted with a 7.62 machine gun for the tank commander. It was a little old, but still packed a pretty good punch. As always, the school lasted for three weeks. I don't know why, but the Legion's schools were in three-week cycles.

A few months had passed, and the next school was motorcycle reconnaissance. They needed to send two people from each platoon to the Legion headquarters at Quartier Montclair for the training. Me and a good friend of mine, Renard, were chosen from our platoon. We were both the same age and had a very strong competitive spirit. The first two weeks of the school was spent learning the very basics of the Husqvarna 125 motorcycle from maintenance to driving and moving in urban environments. The third week was spent out in the field where we would learn land navigation, information gathering, receiving and passing information, and camouflage. The base camp and staging area for the final week was at a training facility called Arta located on the Gulf of Tadjoura, where the legions commando school was held. On our first day, we set up our base camp and performed maintenance on our motorcycles. At the end of the first day, we had a briefing on what was expected of us on this last part of the training and to choose a comrade to conduct the missions with. Naturally, me and Renard shook hands and started prepping our gear for the week ahead.

On one of our first missions, we were given five grid coordinates and a map and needed to locate them together. They said that there would be a Jeep at each coordinate with a sealed envelope. We were to collect the envelope and pass it to the next Jeep at each location in exchange for another envelope. The envelopes were in a special sequence and had something written on them. We weren't allowed to open them, and they needed to be sealed and only opened and read by the instructors in order to get the next message that corresponded with our team's mission.

When our briefing was over, we ran to our bikes and gunned it out of our base camp and into the desert, not having to say a word to each other, but knowing that it was an all-out race between the both of us to see who would get to each coordinate first. It was close, but I was the first one to arrive at the Jeep, and the instructor handed me the first envelope. I stuffed it in my jacket pocket. We checked our map on the hood of the Jeep for the next location. Before I could even fold the map, Renard was jumping on his motorcycle, yelling, "You're not going to beat me this time!" Twisting his throttle down as far as it would go he spun his tires kicking gravel into the air and speeding away down the dirt road. Jumping on my bike and barking, I said, "You bastard!" I kick-started my bike and cranked hard on the throttle fishtailing it out of there, leaving the Jeep in a cloud of dust and gravel. We completed the mission and got all the envelopes in their proper sequence. Renard won the race back to camp on this mission, but I wasn't going to let him win the next one.

The next morning, we were briefed on our next mission, which would be an observation of a road intersection on the Djiboutian highway about forty miles north of the base camp. This would be a night mission that started at 9:00 p.m., and we would have to observe the intersection until 4:00 a.m. before daybreak. We had all day to prep our gear and plot a route through the desert, which would give us the best cover and concealment to a hill overlooking the intersection.

We left our base camp around six that evening to a designated wadi we had chosen for our route, roughly fifteen miles from the intersection we were to observe, that led into a large valley that swept around behind a range of hills overlooking the intersection. We stashed our motorcycles behind some large boulders and camouflaged them with netting and brush. We snuck up the side of the hill and then crawled the last twenty feet to the crest to get a view of the intersection below. We camouflaged our observation post to protect us from both being seen and from the sun, which was still out. We waited into the night, taking turns, watching the intersection in periodic intervals, and sharing rations trying to rest but not really resting at all. The temperature dropped from a daytime of 120°F down to 50°F, having to put our thermal sweaters on and wrap ourselves in our poncho liners. We waited all night until 4:00 a.m., and nothing crossed the intersection not even a herdsman with his cattle.

We gathered our gear, snuck back down the hillside, recovered our motorcycles, and headed back to our base camp on a different route from which we started the mission. Our base camp was located on the coast of the Red Sea and was the location of the French Foreign Legion's commando school called CECAP (Centre d'entrainement au combat d'Arta Plage). The path from the main highway down to the base camp was about fifteen miles, and it snaked down a large wadi system. The ruts of the road were perfect for two motorcycles to race in at full speed.

On this early morning, it was a close race and our bikes were bumping each other on the curves. On one of the S curves, the dirt road hugged the wall of the wadi and horseshoed to the left around a large field of small boulders. As we entered the S curve, I was ahead by half a length, and we were leaning our bikes to our left and into the horseshoe. I was on the outside when I felt Renard kick the side of my bike near the rear tire. I said to myself, So that's how you want to play, you son of a bitch! I was pissed, started kicking his front tire, and tried pushing him into the boulders.

We were at full speed. I swerved hard left to try to make him crash, but he slammed on his brakes at the last minute, and I flew into the boulders. My front tire hit one of the large rocks and threw me into the air. My rear tire hit another rock and threw my ass into the air above my motorcycle. The only contact I had with my bike were my hands, holding on to the handlebars for dear life. I came back down hard on the seat. I missed the pedals with my feet and landed square on my balls, and it felt like they got knocked straight up into my tonsils. It was difficult to maintain the motorcycle up right through the pain, and it was taking all my strength and concentration to keep from crashing.

Out of the corner of my eyes, I could see Renard taking the S curve fast and tight. From the reflection of the headlight on his face, I could see that he was laughing, and that pissed me off even more. I said to myself, Fuck this shit! I cranked the throttle back as far as it would go, and then my bike started bouncing like a crazy bronco just out of the chute.

To my amazement, I made it out of there and onto the dirt road at the other end and far ahead of Renard, beating him back to camp. I jumped off my bike, throwing my helmet to the ground. I ran toward Renard, as he was pulling up, yelling, "Why in the fuck did you kick my bike?"

He was still laughing uncontrollably and choked out. "I didn't mean to kick your bike. I was trying to adjust my body to get ready for the curve, and my foot slipped and hit your bike by accident!" he said while taking off his helmet.

"Then you kicked my front tire, and it twisted in the sand, stopping my bike and almost throwing me over the handlebars!"

I knelt down checking my motorcycle for damage. He hunched his body over the seat of my bike, laughing, and said, "Then I looked up, and you swerved in front of me and went into the rocks. Your ass was flying in the air. That was the funniest thing that I had ever seen. I thought you were going to die for sure!" He was still laughing. "Then while you were bouncing around, I heard your motorcycle rev-up and go faster. It made me laugh so hard I could barely drive my motorcycle! Why did you rev-up and go faster? Weren't you afraid of crashing?"

I replied, "I could see you laughing at me, and it pissed me off. I wanted to beat you even more!"

He then helped me check my bike for damages, laughing the whole time.

We ate breakfast then refueled our motorcycles. We had a few hours before our next mission, so we rested on our cots, talking and laughing about what had happened that morning. They assembled the group and told us that each team would receive their mission from an instructor who was waiting in one of the tents. They called on the first team, and they spent about fifteen to twenty minutes in the tent. They then left on their bikes to start their mission. The instructor waited around thirty minutes then called on the next team. This process happened a couple more times before our team was called, and we were the fifth team to be called out of a group of six.

We entered the tent, and there was an instructor sitting behind a foldout table. The instructor gave us two coordinates and said that one was of our location at the base camp, and the other was of the Jeep that was located past a food relief camp located out in the desert. Then, the instructor handed us a map and told us we had one minute to find both coordinates and to plot a route from our location to the Jeep. The minute was up, and he pulled the map away and stuffed it in a folder, and then from another folder, he handed us a black and white Xerox copy of half of the map and told us we had to draw the rest of the map from memory. We both looked at each other in disbelief, and I started drawing what I remembered. I then handed it to Renard, and he drew what he remembered on the blank side. We exited the tent in full sprint to start the mission. We jumped on our bikes, spinning our tires out of the base camp, traveling up the same wadi we just came down that morning.

Before exiting the wadi and getting onto the main highway, we stopped to take another look at the map. We estimated from our base camp to the UN food relief camp was about forty miles, and then the Jeep was 20 miles past that, which was on the blank part of the map. We gained our bearings and started the mission. We arrived at the UN camp, which was located on the edge of a valley, about an hour later. We stayed in the valley, driving past a cluster of small huts that surrounded the UN tents. As we drove past the camp, people started coming out of the huts with machetes and started running and yelling toward us, throwing rocks.

We hunched low over our bikes and gunned it passed the camp into the narrowing valley. The valley started to get smaller and started to choke with large rocks making it almost impossible to pass. There was a good distance between us and the camp, giving us time to check our map and to look for signs of the other teams coming through this same wadi.

As we were searching for tracks, we could hear the crowd, chanting and coming closer to our location. We could see them now turning a bend in the valley. Putting our helmets on and shaking our hands for good luck, we muscled our motorcycles over the obstacles of rocks and debris, never looking back and followed the wadi until we found the Jeep. We picked up the envelope and asked to see another map to plot a different route to our camp. We arrived back at the base camp completely exhausted that afternoon without any incident. We reentered the tent where the instructor was waiting and handed him the envelope. He opened it and read a small piece of paper to himself, then said, "Good pass," then we exited the tent. We never knew and were never told what was written on those pieces of paper.

Chapter 4

The next day was a Friday, and the day of our final test, which was an endurance test. In the morning, the group was briefed on the mission. We were given three grid coordinates, which were located on the only highway in Djibouti, which snaked North along the coast. We were told that a Jeep with food and fuel would be located at each location and that we would be handed an envelope, which we would have to take to the next Jeep in exchange for another one as before. Our instructors told us not to pass a refueling checkpoint because we would run out of fuel and would be stranded until we were found. The only things we could take with us were two bottles of water, sweater, map, flashlight, and a backpack. Renard and I studied the map, plotted the grid coordinates, and calculated the distance to the last Jeep, which was five hundred miles away from our base camp.

The teams left the base camp in one-hour intervals, and out of the six teams, we were second and left at eight thirty in the morning in the same manner as all the other missions, in a race to see who could get to each checkpoint first. Renard beat me to the first checkpoint. We refueled, ate some C rations, and collected our first envelope; and we were only given fifteen minutes to do it all. We got back on the road and headed north on the highway. The motorcycles didn't go very fast, they only went about ninety mph. Beating me again, we arrived at the second checkpoint without any problems. We exchanged envelopes, refueled, and ate as fast as we could to get back on the highway.

En route to the final checkpoint, Renard was one motorcycle length in front of me and to my left. Everything was going fine, when suddenly, from the corner of my eye, I saw his rear tire bounce straight into the air, almost sending him over his bike. Turning my head and thinking to myself, Holy shit, he's going to… I couldn't even finish the sentence when my rear tire shot into the air, almost sending my ass over the handlebars riding on my front wheel! Amazingly, we were both able to get control of our bikes and land our rear wheels on the ground safely. We looked at each other in amazement and laughed it off as though nothing had happened.

We finally arrived at the third and final checkpoint late in the afternoon and handed the instructor the envelope. He opened it, read the sheet of paper that was inside, and handed us another envelope to return to the instructors at base camp. We refueled and grabbed a bite to eat and started on our journey back to camp. On our way back to the second checkpoint, we discovered what caused us to almost wipe out. When heading from the south to the north on the highway, the road rises, and then dips into a small creek, which was worn away by recent rains. The trench was roughly four feet wide and three feet deep, and when we flew over it, our front tires made it across to the other side, but our rear tires dipped down, hitting the far wall and sending us into the air. We slowly maneuvered around the obstacle and continued on our way.

We arrived at the first checkpoint around 10:30 p.m., refueled, and choked down some bread and paté that was prepared for us by the instructors. Leaving the Jeep in a cloud of dust, we were off again in the allotted fifteen minutes. While on the highway, around midnight, we passed a large clump of bushes and disturbed a flock of doves, which ranged in the hundreds. We slammed into the huge flock at full speed, and it felt like going through a wall. In a large poof, we were covered in blood and feathers! We both had birds flopping around inside of our jackets. We stopped and opened our jackets to let the dying birds out. We both had large welts all over our chest and arms. Putting our gear back on and getting back on our bikes, to continue the mission, we just looked at each other shaking our heads and laughing.

We finally arrived at the base camp around four in the morning and delivered the final envelope to the waiting instructor, and like before, he read what was on the piece of paper and only said, "Good pass!"

We bedded down for the rest of the morning, not being able to sleep, we talked about the entire mission. We stayed up until the last team made it in. The next morning, after breakfast, we started breaking down the camp and were talking to the other teams and found out that they all hit the same trench, almost flipping over their handlebars and riding on their front tires like we did. It's amazing that nobody crashed and got hurt.

The school was over, and we returned back to our units that Saturday afternoon still dusty and dirty from our final mission. Renard and I reported back to our lieutenant, informed him on our performance, and gave him our certificates of completion. During the meeting, he told us that our entire platoon was going to commando school the following month and that our training was going to intensify. There were two physical training sessions, one in the morning and one in the afternoon—for the rest of the month. This will also be followed by a forty-mile forced march one week before going to the commando school. I really liked what I was doing, and I was very proud of being a legionnaire. I was excited about commando school.

On the post that I was stationed on, there was only one phone line that connected us to the outside world, which was in a small telephone booth behind our headquarters office building. There was always a line of legionnaires waiting in the afternoon for their chance to call home. Luckily for me, the perfect opportunity for calling home was around six in the morning, which would be around ten o'clock at night in Texas. So, the telephone booth was always free. The downside to this was that for some reason, the Legion worked five and a half days out of the week, compared to other French forces who only worked five days, which only gave me Sunday mornings to call home.

I called home the next morning after three weeks of silence. I could only imagine how my family felt not hearing from me for long stretches at a time. I tried sending letters and pictures as often as I could, but that was more like once a month. We made small talk, and I told them how my training would intensify in the next couple of months in preparation for and attending the commando school. I apologized to my family for not calling more often than I had been. They were always understanding and never made me feel bad or guilty for not communicating more often than I had been. We said our goodbyes and hung up the phone.

Immediately, our physical training increased from just exercising once in the morning to twice a day—from calisthenics and long runs in the morning to calisthenics and laps in a swimming pool in the afternoon. This lasted for a month until the week before the commando school. We had to complete the final phase of our physical training, which was the forty-mile forced march that our lieutenant scheduled for us. On the morning of the forced march, our lieutenant briefed the platoon on the mission and showed us on a map where our PZ (pickup zone) was designated, which was located a few miles outside the Legion post. The lieutenant stated that we would be picked up by two Puma helicopters at nine that evening and transport the platoon forty miles northwest of that location, showing us coordinates to an LZ (landing zone), which was located high on a mountain range plateau.

Our mission was to patrol back to our post in two nights and one day, searching for hostile forces. We were told to prepare our web gear with the regular combat load of ammunition and two canteens of water, to lighten our rucksacks, and carry the bare minimum for three days; and we would be resupplied with food and water the morning after our first night. I took only a first aid kit, tarp, rope, socks, rations, several bottles of water, and extra ammo.

We marched out of the post at around seven that evening arriving at the PZ an hour before the choppers. We had some time to kill, so a few of us decided to eat some of the rations to put something in our stomachs before the long night ahead. So, 9:00 p.m. rolled around, and you could hear the distinctive sound of two Puma helicopters getting closer in the night. They landed and picked up our thirteen-man team and lifted into the air in a seemingly effortless coordinated motion. We flew banking and weaving within the valleys of the mountain range, making several false insertions before landing at our LZ on top of the large plateau around ten that evening. We exited the choppers and made a hasty 360-security perimeter.

We stayed in security for about fifteen to twenty minutes, so our eyes and ears could get accustomed to the night and our surroundings. After the twenty minutes, the lieutenant called the group together in a tight huddle for a quick briefing and gave one of the corporals an azimuth, pointing in a southeasterly direction, and assigned him as point man for the first night of the mission. It was dark, but the full moon lit up the night sky, and we were able to maneuver between the large rocks and thorny bushes in single file without any problems. The ground was still hot and radiating heat from the day before, which was making us sweat a lot more than anticipated, combined with that, and the grueling pace we had to keep to finish our first twenty miles on time to reach our resupply zone before the blazing sun rose in the sky the next morning. This was a bad sign of things to come!

The night was calm and quiet as we lowered into the valley below on this windless night. The heat radiating from the ground was making us sweat profusely, intensifying everyone's thirst, and making us gulp down our water a lot faster than normal. Around three in the morning, I finished the last drops of water that I had and was craving for more. I asked the guy in front of me and behind me if they had any water, and they both were out too. We put small pebbles in our mouths to keep from getting cottonmouth. A few hours later, we did a security halt and did a quick weapons and personnel check and turned out the entire team was out of water.

At this point, it was around five in the morning, and we still had four to five hours left to reach the resupply point. I had never been so thirsty like this before in my life. The intense thirst which tore at the back of my throat was a pain that I had never felt before. I will never forget that feeling; it has forever been burned into my memory. We finally reached the resupply point around nine in the morning, that first night was grueling and felt like it was never going to end, and to make matters worse, there was no helicopter waiting for us at the resupply point. The sun had been out for a couple of hours now and beating down on us. We hunkered down and set up some hoochs, using camouflaged waterproof polyurethane tarps made for wet weather climates and not the desert.

The tarps did block the sun's rays but increased the heat underneath them. It was so hot the entire team stripped down to their underwear to withstand the heat. It was now noon and still no helicopter. We were so thirsty that we couldn't even eat our rations due to the burning thirst in our throats. Off in the distance, someone spotted two local tribesmen with camels, and we all waved at them to come to our location. We all gathered around them, luckily one of the team members spoke Arabic and asked where the nearest watering hole was. They pointed to a valley, which was several miles away and far to the north.

We didn't want to risk any members of the team to go out and retrieve water from a watering hole not knowing the exact location and risking an ambush from nomads. We asked the tribesmen if they would take our empty water bottles and collect the water for us in exchange for rations and money. They agreed, and we loaded both camels with all our empty water bottles, and they headed in the direction of the distant valley. As they were walking away, one of the tribesmen clasped his hands and praised Allah for the fortune that he had brought them. As we stood there in our underwear, watching them walk away, I too was praising Allah in my head for this great fortune!

It was now three in the afternoon and still no resupply helicopter. Lying underneath our temporary hoochs in 120° F weather was unbearably painful. Soaked in sweat and unable to eat due to the pain in our mouths, we laid there desperately waiting for the resupply helicopter. Then off in the far distance, we could hear the distinct sounds of helicopter blades cutting through the air and coming our way. Jumping into frantic action fueled by our thirst and hunger, we threw our clothes and gear back on and searched desperately into the hot desert sky for the helicopter.

At first, it was a small speck in the sky, which grew larger and louder every minute. I never felt so happy and relieved before in my life. The helicopter landed in an open area about three hundred meters from our position. The team gathered together and unloaded the helicopter of all its supplies and discovered that there was only water and no rations. We asked the crewmen if there was another helicopter bringing the rations, and he said that this was the only resupply for this mission and that the only thing that was requested was water. We were screwed because we still had to give the tribesman what little rations that we had, like we had promised, for fetching the water for us. We distributed the water, and each man got five two-quart bottles. We each inventoried our rations and kept only crackers, candies, sugar, and Kool-Aid packets. We then collected all the can rations and what little money we had for the tribesmen.

Each man chugged one bottle of water and tried to eat what he could from his meager leftover rations. It was now five in the afternoon, and the tribesmen returned as promised with the water. As we unloaded the water, we noticed that the bottles were filled with dark brown water with chunks of mud and gunk floating around inside. After unloading, we gave the two men the rations and the money as promised. Being this far out in the middle of nowhere, the watering hole must have been where rainwater collected in a wash for wild animals to use and where the local tribesmen took their herds of goats and camels. We needed the water no matter what the condition it was in, and it would give each man on the team an extra two bottles of water.

We started filtering the water using our first aid gauze pads as makeshift filters. From one bottle to another, we poured the water through the gauze pads to remove the heavy chunks of mud and silt. After removing the debris, we dumped all of our purification tablets into each bottle to eliminate all the parasites that we could. We then dumped all of our sugar and Kool-Aid packets in each bottle to change the taste and give a little extra energy boost. Each man received two bottles of muddy water, and we all agreed that they would be the very last ones we would drink from our rationed portion.

I was really hoping that we would arrive at the Legion post before having to drink them. We moved out that evening a little after seven, and the weather conditions were exactly the same as the night before—hot and dry with absolutely no wind or cloud cover. The ground felt even hotter than before. We needed to keep the same grueling pace in order to reach the Legion post at nine in the morning to complete the mission on the scheduled time.

As we moved out into the night, I tried real hard not to drink my rations of water, but it was impossible since my throat was killing me, and my body needed the water. Each time I touched my canteen to my chapped lips, I gulped uncontrollably out of instinct. At two in the morning, we stopped to do a weapons and personnel check and to get our bearings. We asked each other what our individual situation was on our water supply, and the entire team had run out of water, even the muddy water was gone. Our thirst was so strong that we couldn't conserve any water even if we tried. We were just too dehydrated. And again, sticking pebbles in our mouths, we moved out into the hot moon lit night.

It was now four in the morning, and we were descending one of the countless ridges when the man in front of me collapsed from dehydration and exhaustion. I tried waking him, but he wasn't responding. I checked his pulse, and he was still alive and yelled for a medic. The medic arrived and immediately administered an IV and explained to our lieutenant that the legionnaire was going to have to be moved down to open area in the valley below to be medevac by helicopter. The lieutenant agreed and stayed on top of the ridge line with the RTO (radiotelephone operator) while the rest of the team carried the unconscious legionnaire down into the creek bed and out to the large open valley on a litter. Before exiting the creek bed, another legionnaire collapsed from dehydration and exhaustion, and he too was given an IV.

We stayed in place and waited for news on the medevac from our lieutenant who was still up on the ridge. An hour had passed, and the lieutenant and RTO descended to our location and said that there was not going to be a medevac by helicopter due to the close proximity of the Legion post only being several miles away. Instead, the post was sending a Jeep to resupply us with water and to evacuate the fallen legionnaires. It was now six in the morning, and the Jeep arrived, and we unloaded the water and loaded the two legionnaires into the vehicle. We started walking out of the valley, and the sun was creeping out from behind one of the mountains and illuminating the area. I immediately knew where we were now. We had trained there before in the past and realized that the post was only about five miles away. The Jeep passed us and left us in a cloud of dust. Only having several hours left to complete the mission, we started to jog out of the valley to reach the Legion post on time.

Running up the hill, that the post was located on, and through the front gates stopping at our motor pool, with a lot of time to spare, the mission was over. We dropped all our gear, and everyone practically ripped their BDU tops off in complete exhaustion to cool off. The whole team was hunched over looking at the ground with their hands on their knees, trying to catch their breath with big heavy gulps of air.

Once we caught our breaths, we stood up and looked at each other in complete amazement. We touched each other's sunken faces and protruding cheekbones. We all had lost between fifteen to twenty pounds a person in the two-day ordeal. The post medics brought us more bottled water and boxes of rations. We sat down, ate, and discussed what had gone wrong and what we had done right on the mission. As a group, we considered it a success. It was Wednesday, and the commando school started the following Monday and only had four days to pack the pounds back that we had lost on the patrol. So, for four days, we gorged on junk food, cakes, sodas, and pretty much anything we could get a hold of to regain the fat that we had lost.

Chapter 5

Monday arrived, and the entire platoon with other personnel from the company, including the men who collapsed from dehydration, was shipped off to commando school, which was located on the Gulf Coast of Tadjoura near the Red Sea in the same camp where the motorcycle reconnaissance school was held.

For the first two weeks of commando school, our daily routines were mixed with hand-to-hand combat and individual and team obstacle courses. We learned beach infiltration by rubber boat, and we also learned how to recon and attack enemy positions and equipment. The one thing that still sticks to my mind to this very day is the hand-to-hand combat. We started every morning before dawn and breakfast with an hour to two hours of physical fitness training and hand-to-hand combat. We were paired up with sparring partners and shown several offensive and defensive techniques. The objective of the instructor was to teach you how to use the technique in full speed real combat situations and not to pull any punches.

When you grabbed your sparring partner and flipped him to the ground with the technique that was shown, you are expected to use all your energy to throw him, and in response, your sparring partner was to use the technique that was shown to fall and absorb the shock. Punches were thrown at full speed and needed to be defended against correctly, if not, you were getting a black eye for breakfast. If the techniques weren't being performed properly or at full speed, the instructors would reteach that technique on the individual and show no mercy. The training was conducted on a gravel beach covered with large rocks near the school, and every time you were thrown to the ground, you felt every rock dig deep into your back, stomach, thighs, or whatever part of your body you fell on. The beach was unforgiving.

On the third week, we practiced more raiding techniques and movement to contact patrols, and we also practiced insertions by helicopter and rubber boat. We had a different mission every night with two to three objectives per mission, lasting the entire night each night, and resting during the day. On our last mission, a day before the final three-day forced march—which incorporated all the things we had learned in the school from raids to patrols, overcoming obstacles, explosives, hand-to-hand combat, and POW survival—we were to infiltrate a cove at dawn by boat and destroy two enemy vehicles using all the remaining C4 that we had leftover from the school with timed fuses. We would then march back to the school that morning, which was five miles away from the cove.

After finishing our last patrol, we moved down to the beach from the mountains where the rubber boats and instructors were waiting for us. We shoved off, paddling into the choppy gulf, all in a row, and quietly landed in the cove around five in the morning just before dawn. We conducted our infiltration of the beachhead and snuck our way to the two burnt out vehicles. As we were doing this, the instructors started paddling the rubber boats back to base camp. We unloaded the C4 and stacked all the pieces under both chassis and motor compartments. We daisy chained all the pieces together, and then we piled whatever debris we could find on top of the vehicles to dampen the explosion because we knew there was a lot of C4 to destroy.

We set the time fuse to go off in fifteen minutes, thinking that would give us enough time to hike over the next hill and find cover. Our timing was way off, the hill was larger than we expected, and three quarters on the way up the side of the hill, the vehicles exploded simultaneously with one loud ear-splitting ground shaking boom, sending all the debris and large chunks of metal into the air over our heads. Looking up, we could see the pieces of motor, doors, and unrecognizable chunks of metal fly up then float for a few seconds then start falling down toward us. Someone yelled, "Run!"

We all broke rank and started running up toward the crest of the hill to get to the other side, and safely to the beach below. Large pieces of metal were falling all around us, and I could see people dodging around pieces that had landed directly in front of them.

We crested the hill, continued running down, and found cover behind some large boulders near the beach. Peeking from behind a boulder, I could see a large cloud of smoke, pushing its way into the sky from behind the hill. We gathered ourselves to check for injuries, but everyone was okay, just a few bumps and bruises among us. We marched back and rested for the remainder of the day before we started the three-day testing phase of the commando school that evening.

We arrived back at our base camp around nine, ate breakfast, and rested for about four hours that morning, waking up at one in the afternoon to eat again and prepare our equipment for the next three days. Around four in the afternoon, the platoon was gathered for a mission report for the evening's tasks. We were told that we would be picked up by helicopter and infiltrated into an area controlled by enemy forces to knockout their radio communications tower located on top of a mountain. We then were to exfiltrate the enemy position by rappelling down the side of the mountain, where the communications tower was located, and then search for a waiting convoy for resupply. Shortly after the mission report, we collected our gear and moved out to the designated PZ on the beachhead near the camp. We waited for several hours in a 360-security position until, finally, three helicopters arrived, landing near our location sometime after 7:00 p.m.

We lifted off and headed in a westerly direction for about an hour, making several false insertions, and finally landing in a designated LZ a couple valleys away from the mountain where the radio station was located. We marched for several hours in the hot and dark night in and out the valleys until finally locating and sneaking up to the radio station. We prepared two teams, one to provide cover fire, and another to assault the compound. We attacked the station with small arms and grenades finishing up around one in the morning. After destroying the radio station, we were led by an instructor outside the compound to the rappelling site. They led us down a ravine with a sharp cliff, it was pitch-black, and we couldn't see anything but chemlights on the trail leading to the rappelling point. We put on our rappelling harnesses and descended one by one over the side of the mountain into the darkness below.

We had all our equipment on as we rappelled down the face of the cliff. I was third in the group to go, and I hooked up and let myself down over the side. I couldn't see anything, and I couldn't even touch the wall of the cliff with my feet. I couldn't judge the distance to the ground. It felt like it was taking forever to descend, and then all of a sudden, I landed on the ground square on my ass. I recovered immediately and set up a security position to wait for the rest of the platoon. After the entire platoon descended, we did a headcount, an equipment check, and plotted a course to the direction of the waiting convoy. We found the trucks at daybreak and got resupplied with food, water, and ammo. While eating our rations, the instructors briefed us on our next mission. We were to get helicoptered out, dropped off into a valley, march up over several mountains, and attack and eliminate all hostiles in a small village, located in a large valley, at dawn.

The trucks stayed in place, and we set up security resting in their shade for the rest of the day. In the afternoon, at around five, we marched to a nearby PZ and waited for the helicopters. As we were walking to the pickup zone, the resupply convoy left for our next rendezvous point. It wasn't long before the Puma helicopters arrived. We boarded quickly and flew into the air. It wasn't a long flight, only staying in the air for about thirty to forty minutes, and arriving at our landing zone at dusk. We started on our march to the east toward the mountains, shortly after the helicopters took off, which lasted all night. We crested the mountain at daybreak, and the sun was rising to the east directly in front of us.

We could see the village down below in the valley, its buildings looked like small blocks in the sand. Realizing we still had a long way to go, we pushed down the mountain at a faster pace. The descent lasted for several hours, and we were almost at the bottom of the mountain when I tripped on a loose rock, lost my footing, and felt and heard a snap from my left foot. From the sharp pain, I knew I had broken my little toe. The pain was incredible, but I couldn't stop since we still had several miles to the objective. We made it to the village, attacked, and cleared the buildings around midday. I limped across the dusty village, set up security, and just fell to the ground to take the weight off my foot it was killing me, but the mission wasn't over yet, and I couldn't do or say anything until the mission was complete.

A cease-fire was called, and we were told to hold in our security positions. The resupply convoy rolled through the dusty road and parked at the west end of the village. A medic went to each man at their position to see if they needed medical attention. When he arrived at my position, I told him that I thought my toe was broken, and he asked me to take off my boot and confirmed that my toe was broken. He told me that I had one of two options. One was to get on one of the resupply trucks and go back to the commando school and get medical attention, but in doing so that meant I would be quitting the school, which meant I would have to repeat the course later. The second option was to take painkillers to complete the final night and day missions of the exercise and complete and finish the commando school.

I chose to take the pain pills. I didn't want to go through this shit again. The medic gave me a pill bottle filled with large white pills, which I had never seen before, and instructed me to take one pill an hour before we started the mission and to take one pill every time the pain came back. After that, I limped to our next mission briefing. The mission was to march all night to an enemy headquarters and attack and kill all enemy personnel. We were then to carry a wounded legionnaire on a litter back to the commando school, which was two miles away from the enemy headquarters. I was worried that I wasn't going to make it. We rested for the remainder of the afternoon in our security positions. I was on my back, underneath a bush, with my left foot propped up on a rock and using my rucksack as a pillow. My foot was throbbing with pain as I lay there in the burning sun underneath that small bush. I still had a few hours before I could take the first pill.

I rested there, biting on my lower lip, trying to ignore the pain. We were one hour out from our third and final mission, and I took the first pill, not really expecting the pain to go away. Around thirty to forty minutes passed, and I couldn't feel any pain at all. I slipped my boot back on and tightened my laces extra tight, so my foot wouldn't move around in my boot. I stood up, walked around, and was amazed that there was no pain. It was now around six in the evening, and we assembled in single file and started the mission. I was walking as if there was nothing wrong with my foot. I was so relieved. We marched as always, all night, and with few stops. Every time I felt the pain start to come back, which was every two to three hours, I would take one of those pills, and the pain was gone within thirty minutes.

We arrived and attacked the mock enemy headquarters around five in the morning just before daybreak. After securing the headquarters we set up security and waited for the next mission, which was to carry a wounded soldier back to the commando school. After getting a headcount, an equipment, and ammo check, one of the instructors—monitoring our attack on the headquarters—went to each squad, which was four squads with seven people per squad, and pointed to one person in each squad and said, "You're wounded." It wasn't me from my squad, who was designated to be the wounded soldier, bummer! Each squad was handed a litter and told to start the mission. I felt the pain start to come back, and I took my last pill. Each team headed for the commando school, which was about two miles southeast of the mock enemy headquarters, running at a slow jog and then stopping every several hundred yards to lower the casualty and to switch men and positions on the litter to give our arms a rest.

The entire platoon arrived at the commando school with all four men still safe in their litters and not injured. We finished, and everyone was happy and shaking each other's hands and congratulating each other for completing the commando school, or so we thought. Six instructors came out from around one of the buildings with assault rifles drawn, yelling at us, "Drop your weapons, and take off all of your gear. You are now POWs!"

We were told to take both laces off our boots and to take our T-shirts off and to put our BDU tops back on. With laces and T-shirts in our hands, we were led to a large pit at gunpoint. The pit was large enough to put three tanks in it side-by-side. The instructors blindfolded us with our T-shirts, and then told us to lay on our stomachs with our hands behind our backs. After lying down, the instructors went to each man and hogtied our hands and feet with our bootlaces. We lay there in the morning sun and waited. They left us there for a couple of hours, and the sun started to get hotter.

The team was silent. I could only hear the instructor's boots walking up and down the ranks of the POWs. Several more hours passed before I heard an instructor untie the first group of guys and shuffle them off out of the pit. It seemed like they were getting a group every thirty to forty minutes, but I couldn't really tell. The pain pills had worn off about an hour into the pit. I didn't know what time it was, but I could feel the sun burning my back at an eleven or twelve o'clock position. I heard someone walk toward me and untie my hands and feet and told me to get up with three or four other guys. We were still blindfolded, and they lined us up in single file and told us to put both hands on the shoulders of the man in front of us. I then felt someone put their hands on my shoulders. My foot was throbbing, and I was limping really badly by now.

They marched us into a room that was freezing cold and felt like a meat locker. From underneath my blindfold, I could see the concrete floor. We were led around a makeshift table, which was about a foot off the ground, made of plywood and bricks. They told us to stop face the table, get down on our knees, lean forward, and place our foreheads on the table. They then retied our hands behind our backs. They told us if we moved that we would be beaten. Then they started pouring buckets filled with water and ice on our backs. The shock of going from a hundred-degree heat outside to what felt like thirty degrees in an instant was incredible on your body. I couldn't even feel the pain in my foot anymore. I started shaking really bad, and then I got kicked on my side, sending me to the ground. They then started pouring water on me and yelling at me while I was down. I got up as fast as I could and put my forehead back on the table. Then I heard someone else get kicked to the ground with a loud moan. I could hear him scramble to his knees, put his forehead on the table with a thump, and then there was silence.

I heard one of the instructors grab one of the guys and pulled him to his feet, saying, "Let's go!" Then the door swung open, and I could see a ray of sunlight bounce off the table and the shadow of both the legionnaire and instructor walk outside from under the slit in my blindfold. A few minutes later, they grabbed another guy. It was too cold, and we couldn't control our bodies from shaking. They also kept kicking us to the ground. Then I heard one of the instructors walk behind me, grabbed me by the collar of my jacket, and yelled, "On your feet!" I heard the door swing open. He pushed me out into the hot sun, untied my hands, and then yanked the blindfold off my head. My eyes squinted from the bright sun.

Not seeing another instructor from the glare, he smacked me across the left side of my head with boxing mitts, yelling, "Fight, punch!" He then smacked me on the right side of my head. Shaking my head, I punched the mitts with what little energy I had, and then he yelled, "Front roll punch, then front kick!"

I rolled forward, and then I gave a jab, followed with a low front kick. My body started to warm up, and my foot started hurting again. The instructor explained to me that there will be ten stations with an attacker or a victim at each station, and I had to use a defensive or offensive technique that I had learned at the school.

We jogged to each station all the while having to punch and kick the instructor's pads and use a fighting technique at each station. After completing the final station, the instructor jogged me to the beach where I saw the rest of my comrades resting in the water and gave me one last command "Front roll into the ocean!"

I rolled into the ocean and collapsed from exhaustion. I just lay there with my body halfway in the ocean and on the beach. That was the most intense three weeks of my legion life. It was harder than the farm. The platoon completed the school, and each man that passed received the coveted commando badge, which was of an eagle clutching the brigade's insignia and a sword running through from behind.

Chapter 6

Finally, we were finished with all our training, and when we got back to garrison, the lieutenant gathered the platoon together and said that he wanted the privates to concentrate on getting rank. He said that in six months, there was going to be a corporal's course coming up and that he wanted to send a couple of us through the course. I was excited. Everything was going just as I planned, slowly but surely, everything was coming together. A couple of months passed, and my foot healed nicely. We were spending a lot of time back at garrison, and we would go out to the field for a couple of days every other week and practice patrolling and raids, not much was going on. Then, one day, the entire 13th Demi-brigade was put on high alert.

Our lieutenant briefed us and said that the Ethiopian government was fighting rebel forces trying to topple its government. The rebels had successfully captured a port city that was next to the border and that the Ethiopian forces were massing along the border in order to push into Djibouti and outflank the rebels and attack the city from the south. The lieutenant told us that the commander of the French forces in Djibouti had sent a message to the Ethiopian government that stated if any Ethiopian military personnel crossed the border, it would do battle with the 13th Demi-brigade of the French Foreign Legion. We were told that our mission was simple, and it was to not allow any Ethiopian forces to cross the border into Djibouti and that we were to hold our positions at all costs. Within a couple of hours, the entire recon company was fully loaded with food, water, and ammunition. The convoy consisted of twelve ERC

90's light armored tanks and twelve Jeeps fitted with .50 caliber machineguns and supply trucks. I was a gunner on one of the Jeeps.

We got word that the main body of the brigade was on the road and headed toward our post. We then received word to move out at noon before the main body and provide recon on the terrain and enemy. Our company headed due north on the main highway toward the border of Ethiopia. We drove all afternoon and into the night, arriving at our designated rendezvous point, in the open desert, early the next morning. We were instructed to line all of the tanks horizontally facing north toward the border with a seventy to one-hundred-meter space between each tank, leaving enough room for the Jeeps, mounted with the 50 caliber, to fit in between them. We pointed all our weapons north fully locked and loaded. We were told to attack any and all Ethiopian forces that crossed into Djibouti. I wasn't scared this time around, like I was in the Gulf War, I was more mature and a lot calmer. I knew exactly what I had to do to stay alive.

The main body of the brigade arrived that afternoon, and they split the remaining three infantry companies into two large companies. One company was placed past our farthest western position, and the other company was placed past our farthest eastern position, lining their armored personnel carriers and Jeeps in the same manner as we did. Our lieutenant reported back to headquarters that there was no sign of the enemy. Our lieutenant reported back to us over the radio reminding us that we were to hold our positions at all costs.

The troop strength of the 13th Demi-brigade totaled to about six hundred legionnaires, and the Ethiopians had massed a force, estimated to be around two thousand soldiers, along the border, ready to sweep into Djibouti and outflank the rebel forces from the South. We were outnumbered but not outgunned. The French Air Force was flying daily sorties low and close to the border to intimidate the Ethiopians. We waited for an entire week in our positions ready to do combat. Toward the end of the week, we got word over the radio from our lieutenant that the Ethiopian military was pulling its forces from the border and was going to attack the city straight on. I guess they felt it was wiser to fight one foe than to have to fight two.

The show of force worked, and we won the conflict without having to fire a single shot. We celebrated with handshakes and pats on our backs, and then we opened a bottle of wine. We all toasted and drank out of our canteen cups and sang our company's marching song in defiance toward the border. We returned to garrison that Friday afternoon, and good thing too, we really wanted to rest that weekend.

That Saturday morning, I snuck into our posts telephone booth and called home to my family to let them know what was going on all week and let them know why I haven't been in touch. My father answered the phone, and we chatted about little things here and there. I explained to him that we had been dispatched to block an Ethiopian force from infiltrating into Djibouti territory, and that they were too scared to cross the border. "That's great, son," he said.

He didn't sound like his usual self throughout the entire conversation. I knew something was wrong, and I didn't want to press the issue. He sounded upset, so I asked to speak to Mom and my little brother, but he told me that they had just left to go to the grocery store just before I called. "I'll call back in about an hour," I told him and expecting an "I'll let them know" or "I'll tell them that you'll be calling back" kind of response, instead there was a long pause, and I thought the phone had hung up. "Dad, are you still there?"

"Son, we have some bad news," he replied, and from the sadness in the tone of his voice, I knew something was seriously wrong.

My left hand tightened on the telephone receiver, and my knees started shaking with fear.

"Your mother has been visiting these doctors, and they had been running some tests on her for the last several months. They told us that she was going to need heart surgery and that her kidneys were failing. If she survived heart surgery, she would have to undergo another surgery to prepare her for dialysis, and if she doesn't agree to get these surgeries that the doctors told her, she would live no longer than a year."

My heart sank into my chest completely shattered. Then he said, "Your mother didn't want you to find out about what was going on with her, she didn't want you to worry about her."

I said to my father, "I need to know everything that is going on over there at all times. Please don't keep anything from me this time around, okay? Thanks for telling me, and on Monday, I'm going to request to speak to the captain and ask to take leave. Don't worry, I'll be home as soon as possible."

Then my father said, with an upset voice, "Please come home soon, son, I can't go through this without you here by our side as a family."

I reassured him not to worry and that I would be home as quickly as I can no matter what. After hanging up the phone, I walked out of the company headquarters and followed the chain-link fence that surrounded the garrison and stared out into the desert. I had never felt so hopeless before in my life like I did that day. I didn't know what the hell I was going to do. Not again! I thought to myself. I can't let my family down like I did before in the Gulf War and not be there for them! I had to figure something out, but what? I already knew what the captain was going to tell me, that a legionnaire is not allowed to take leave overseas in his first five years of enlistment. I only had two and half years into my contract and would need to wait another two and half years before I was able to take leave overseas. My mother only had one year to live if she didn't undergo the surgeries.

I didn't know what to do, my passport was confiscated when I joined the Legion, and I wouldn't be able to touch it until the end of my enlistment. Then it clicked in my head, The US Embassy! They have to help me. I'm an American! I thought to myself. Yeah, but then again, I'm not the typical blond-haired blue-eyed American. I'm Hispanic with black hair and dark brown eyes, even the local Djiboutian people didn't believe that I was an American, they always called me Algerian. I still had to give it a try once they heard my American accent, they had to believe me.

I left the garrison that same morning, grabbed a taxi, and headed straight for the US Embassy in the capital. When I arrived at the embassy, I had to wait in line to speak to the only clerk working that day sitting behind a heavily windowed counter, who happened to be a white guy. Oh great! I thought to myself.

I explained to him that I was in the Legion and told him that my mother was very sick, and I needed to get my passport to take leave and visit my family. He folded his arms and leaned back, squinting his eyes, and looked me up and down, staring at my Legion uniform and kepi. He then asked in a sarcastic tone, "Where did you learn to speak English so good?"

I was pissed. "Look, man, I'm from San Marcos, Texas. I've lived there all my life, it's a small town just south of Austin. I'll show you on a map if you want, I'm telling you the truth, I'm an American!"

Then he said, "San Marcos, Texas, huh?"

I responded with a pissed off tone. "Yeah, San Marcos, Texas!"

Then he told me, "If you're really an American, I'm going to need a birth certificate, social security card, and a state of Texas picture ID or driver's license with an address from back home on it."

I said, "Thanks, man," and as I was turning away, the clerk said, "Hey, I'm from Dallas."

Turning back, I spit out in amazement, "No shit!"

He said with a smile, "Yeah, no shit, and don't forget a picture for your passport and expect three weeks for the background check, and if all goes well, I'll make sure to push your paperwork before the people trying to get visas."

I said, "Thanks," and breathed a sigh of relief as I walked out of the embassy. The next day was Sunday, and I called home and told my mom that I knew what was going on with her medical condition. I told her I was sorry for leaving her again and that I would be home soon to be by her side. I told her I needed her to find my birth certificate, social security card, and one of my Texas IDs with my picture on it and to ship it to me as fast as she could. I reassured her not to worry that I was going to be home soon no matter what. We said our tearful goodbyes and hung up the phone.

Monday morning arrived, and I requested to see the captain. As I predicted, he refused my request to take leave. I was desperate, and I needed to do something. I couldn't let my mother or father down. I loved the Legion, but I loved of my family more. I couldn't let them down again, not this time. The envelope, which my mother sent me with all of my documentation, arrived the following week. It was now mid-November of '98, and I took all the paperwork immediately to the US Embassy. I met with the guy from Dallas, telling me again that the entire process from background check to processing the passport would take around three weeks and reassured me that he would push my paperwork before the other people trying to get their visas. I told the guy thanks for believing in me and for helping me out. Next, I drained my bank account, which the Legion had within the brigade, and withdrew $10,000. I wired $5000 home and kept the other $5000 for a plane ticket and travel expenses. I immediately bought a one-way ticket for Austin, Texas, dated for the end of December from a local travel agent who I had to bribe. The plan was set in motion, and now all I had to do was sit and wait for a few weeks for my passport to arrive, get it stamped by the travel bureau of Djibouti, jump on a plane, and go home, easy enough.

I started to get really cocky and bold, thinking that I had outsmarted the Legion. I started carrying a flask of whiskey with me everywhere I went to celebrate my ingenious plan. I walked around with a big shit eating grin on my face because no one knew of my plan. I kept everything secret. It was the beginning of December now, and it was our platoon's turn to pull a twenty-four-hour guard shift on the garrison. There were a total of twelve legionnaires and a sergeant of the guard on a twenty-four-hour shift.

They stationed two legionnaires at the front gate, one legionnaire roving the perimeter, and one legionnaire at the ammo depot. The changing of the guard was every morning at five. Then after changing of the guard, each shift was two hours long, and when you weren't on your shift, you rested for six hours.

I was chosen for the roving guard, and one of my shifts was from 11:00 p.m. to 1:00 a.m. The uniform for the roving guard was combat fatigues, loadbearing vest, rifle with one full magazine of ammunition, and green beret, but I added another very important piece of equipment, for me at the time, my flask. I didn't go anywhere without that damn thing. I walked the border of the garrison, drinking out of the flask periodically, and thinking of my mom back home. I was so depressed at the time that I couldn't think straight. The whiskey calmed my nerves.

Toward the end of my shift, the sergeant of the guard had reported to the headquarters building on one of his quarterly reports. I was unaware that he had gone to headquarters. I thought I was all alone roving the garrison in the dark. The sergeant was returning to the guard shack, walking alongside the same barracks I was walking on and traveling in the same direction as I was but on the opposite side of the building. I passed the row of barracks, just before he did, and turned left, tipping the flask back into my mouth as I rounded the corner. I felt something swing at my face, not knowing it was the sergeant, snatching the flask out of my hand. Acting out of pure instinct, I pushed him to the ground and unslung my rifle and pointed it at him. Helping him get up off the ground, he yelled at me, "Drinking on duty!"

I tried to apologize, but he was too angry and yelled at me, saying, "You're reporting to the captain first thing in the morning after guard duty!"

He stomped off in the direction of the guard shack. I reported immediately to the captain that morning, and man was he pissed. He didn't tolerate drinking on duty and especially someone touching one of his NCOs. He wanted to make an example out of me and sentenced me to five weeks in jail and hard labor. My release date was scheduled for the end of January, my whole plan was getting flushed down the toilet, and there was nothing I could do about it. You really fucked up now! I told myself.

I reported to jail immediately after the captain sentenced me that morning. The Legion still used jails and hard labor as a form of punishment to discipline unruly legionnaires. The jail was located behind the guard shack and housed a maximum of ten prisoners. It consisted of ten bunks stacked two high with one solid iron door and one small window with bars, and no screen. The window was opened to the outside, letting mosquitoes fly in and out freely all night. Each man was issued one white sheet cover and a pillow. I remember every night I tried covering every inch of my body to protect against the mosquitoes, but it didn't help, they were always able to sting through the sheets, it was hell getting a decent night's rest. At the time, I shared the jail with five other legionnaires. We reported every morning to the company headquarters at 5:00 a.m. and the sergeant in charge, for that day, would pass out different duties to each legionnaire.

On my first day, I was paired up with a Romanian guy, and we were assigned to spread gravel around the parade grounds. They gave us shovels and a wheelbarrow and marched us to the parade grounds. When we arrived, there was no gravel there, I asked, "What gravel, Sergeant?" The sergeant looked at me with a smirk and said, "Don't worry, we have dump trucks coming loaded with gravel just for you two guys!"

Me and the Romanian looked at each other in an oh fuck kind of way, and said, "Dump trucks!" And within thirty minutes, the two trucks rumbled up and dropped their loads of gravel near the parade grounds, the two piles were taller than us. We started shoveling gravel into the wheelbarrow, pushing it to the farthest points of the parade grounds, and started swinging gravel evenly all around. This is not too bad, I thought to myself, all we have to do is keep a slow steady pace, and we could do this for as long we had to. We worked all day in the blazing sun not allowed to take breaks, and we were only allowed to take breaks for lunch and dinner. The prison uniform was a French GAO shirt (which was sleeveless and open down the sides to let air in and out freely), shorts with combat boots, and boonie hat. We took our shirts off and applied sunscreen, but it didn't help, our heavy sweating just washed it off, and we still got burned.

They stopped us at ten o'clock that night and marched us back to jail to take a quick shower. We had to be in our bunks by 10:30 p.m. I lay there in my bunk, underneath my sheet, trying to fend off mosquitoes, wondering what I was going to do to not miss my flight at the end of the month. I had to do something, but what? I didn't know. The only thing I could do was escape jail and hide in the capital of Djibouti for a couple weeks, wait for my passport to arrive, and jump on the plane. All week we worked on the parade grounds.

While I was working, I was figuring out a plan to escape. I had gotten several different ideas in my head, but none of them seemed successful to me at the time, so I didn't do anything. And by Saturday afternoon, of my first week in jail and slinging gravel, I was completely frustrated and finally made up my mind that tonight's the night I need to break out.

My plan was to wait until eight o'clock, go up to my barracks, pack my duffel bag, and jump the fence to find a taxi and head to the capital. Quick and easy, I thought to myself. Eight o'clock rolled around, and I snuck up to my barracks and packed one of my duffel bags with civilian clothes. I then grabbed the rest of the money I had stashed away. Due to it being Saturday, the entire company was on pass, and there was nobody in the barracks except for a good friend of mine, who never went out much, a Russian named Ignotov. He walked in while I was packing my duffel bag, and this startled me. He asked me what I was doing, but I told him that I couldn't tell him right now and asked him if he could take the duffel bag, get a taxi, and wait for me four or five miles down the highway. I would explain everything to him once we arrived safely at a hotel in the capital. He was a good person and never gave what I was doing a second thought. I think he knew exactly what I was doing and wanted to help.

He agreed, took my duffel bag to the front gates, and got a taxi. I grabbed a wool blanket, snuck out to the back fence of the garrison, hid behind some trash cans, and waited for the roving guard to pass. The back of the garrison faced a wadi system that pointed south toward the capital and ran parallel to the highway. The guard passed, and I waited until he was out of sight and threw the wool blanket over the fence, covering the concertina wire, and climbed over into the wadi. I ran for what I thought was four miles and climbed up the cliff wall to poke my head over the rim to look for the taxi. It was waiting for me a couple miles down the road. I pulled myself out of the wadi and sprinted toward the taxi, dodging bushes and rocks the whole way there. I jumped in the back seat, and Ignotov was waiting in the front seat with the driver. The taxi driver gave us both a strange look, and I told him that if he wanted a good tip that he would keep his mouth shut and drive to the nearest hotel in the capital. Ignotov said with a loud voice, "Drive!"

On the way to the capital, I changed into civilian clothing. We arrived at a hotel, and I asked the driver if $300 sounded like a good tip. His eyes widened, and he nodded his head, saying in excitement,

"Yes!" Then I told him that the only thing he had to do was forget about tonight and not to say a word to anyone. He agreed, and I gave him the money. I rented a room, and while inside, I explained to Ignotov about my mother's condition and what I was planning on doing. He asked me, "How long do you plan on staying at this hotel?"

"Not for very long. I plan on moving around to different hotels every second or third day," I said.

"That's a very bad idea. You'd eventually be seen, and if the Legion puts a ransom on your head, you'd be ratted out by the locals," he told me.

"That's the only idea I have, I have no other choice, the embassy won't let me stay at their facilities."

Then he told me about these Russian civilian airplane mechanics that he met a few months before who were working for the Djiboutian government and had a house near the airport. He said that they would help me out but for a price, seeing how they were hurting for money. It sounded like a good idea, and I agreed to meet with those guys. Ignotov stayed in the hotel that night, and the next morning after breakfast, we got a taxi and drove to the neighborhood, which was about a mile away from the international airport in Djibouti.

When we arrived, we found those guys in a worse predicament than I was in. They had no electricity; no running water, and they were stealing both from their neighbors. They welcomed me in, and we sat down at the kitchen table. Ignotov translated for us, talked about our situations, and discussed how we could help each other. I told them that if they allowed me to stay in the house for two weeks, until I could catch my flight, that I would buy all the food and bottled water for the house, giving them the opportunity to save some money. At the end of the two weeks, I would give them $500 for helping me out. We all agreed on the deal and shook hands. I walked Ignotov to the front gate, where the taxi was waiting, and thanked him for helping me and tried to give him some money, but he refused and told me that I was going to need it. He was a good guy and genuinely just wanted to help me out, still to this day, I wonder why he helped me. We shook hands and said our goodbyes. He got in the taxi and drove off. I never saw him again.

The five Russian men were stranded in the country. I think the Djiboutian government promised them a lot of money to work on their military aircraft but were barely giving them enough money to survive off, let alone to save enough money to leave. That evening, we celebrated the deal by drinking something they called "The Spirit." It was poured out of one of those old moonshine jugs and into coffee cups, and it smelled just like vodka. We drank it straight.

We drank all night until we emptied the gallon jug, and I passed out on the living room floor near my duffel bag. The next day, one of the guys walked in with the jug, where I was sleeping, and woke me up, saying, "Spirit! Spirit!" waving the jug at me. Knowing exactly what he wanted, I stood up to give him money, and said, "Spirit, beer, food!" He understood what I was saying and went into town.

The rest of the guys wanted to show me their Russian movie collection and Russian cassette tapes. I didn't understand anything they were showing me. A couple hours later, the guy I gave the money to showed up with a case of beer, a couple sacks of groceries, and a gallon of rubbing alcohol. He then walked into the kitchen, setting everything on the table. I thought to myself, Maybe he forgot the vodka. He grabbed the empty moonshine jug and started pouring the rubbing alcohol into it. In amazement, I pointed to the rubbing alcohol and said, "No vodka?"

The Russian guy said, "No vodka, spirit!"

Holy shit, we were drinking rubbing alcohol all night! Fuck my life! I thought to myself.

It was extremely difficult communicating with those guys since not one of them spoke English, French, or Spanish. On the second day, one of the guys brought me a stack of French magazines, opened one of them up, and said in a bold voice, "English!"

I squinted my eyes, not understanding what he wanted. He then asked in a more curious voice, "English?" and pointed to a picture of a car.

Oh, he wants me to say it in English. So, I said, "A car."

He repeated, "Acar."

I said very slowly, "No. A car!"

He gave me a funny look. I took the magazine from his hand and circled the picture with my finger and said in a normal tone, "Car."

He nodded and said the word, "car," then he handed me a notebook and motioned with the pen to write the word, "car." I wrote it down, then he copied the word underneath it. And so, for the next couple of days, I tried to teach them some English. They would come up to me and point to pictures in magazines, and I would say the word and write it down for them. They would study it between each other.

Chapter 7

I stayed in the house the entire time only to check on the status of my passport at the embassy. I always wore a baseball cap with sunglasses (FYI—I used that disguise way before the Avengers ever did!), and I also grew my goatee out and tried to limit my exposure time around the locals. Every time I went into town, I took a taxi and went straight to the embassy and back and nowhere else. On the road, I would see trucks full of legionnaires, roaming the streets, searching for me. I went out on Monday of the second week, hoping that my passport would be ready because my flight was scheduled for that Friday. Sure enough, my passport still hadn't arrived, and they told me that it would possibly arrive the next week or the following week. I was pissed! I couldn't believe it I had to wait another two weeks. I was going to miss my flight. I went back to the house totally bummed out. I was getting frustrated being stuck in that house with five other people and not understanding a single thing they were saying. Every evening, they wanted me to sit down and watch old Russian VHS movies that had a lot of communist propaganda in them all the while drinking their "Spirit." It was driving me crazy. I went to bed early every night, not wanting to watch those movies, not really a bed, but a spot in the dining room area on the floor next to my duffel bag.

The next morning, I awoke still frustrated from the day before. I just needed to get out of the house, it was driving me crazy. So, against my plan of limiting my exposure time, I decided to go to the embassy again. Instead of getting a street kid to go find a taxi and have it sent to the house for a couple bucks, like I always did, I went myself to find a taxi and stepped out into the street and started walking toward the main road where all the taxis were located. I just wanted to get away and rethink my situation. The main road was about three quarters of a mile from the house and gave me some time to think and get some fresh air. I ran both scenarios in my head. If the Legion caught me, I would surely be beaten, and I would certainly get a three to four-month prison sentence and hard labor. Then I thought to myself, But I could be home this weekend if they don't catch me. I guess not knowing how my situation was going to turn out is what stressed me out more than not understanding what those guys were saying at the house. I found a taxi and asked him to drive around the city and play some music for a while. I needed to clear my head. He drove around for about thirty minutes then started pointing at his fuel gauge, so I asked him to take me to the embassy. I needed to check again just to satisfy my anxiousness.

I went to the front counter and waited for about fifteen minutes in line. The guy from Dallas was working that day, and as soon as he saw me walk up to the window, he smiled and handed me my passport. "Holy shit!" I said loudly. "It worked."

He said, "I pushed your paperwork before everyone else's, and it actually worked."

I was so excited that I spit out, "I owe you a lot, and I don't know how I'm going to repay you!"

He just replied in a grateful manner, "Don't worry about it, just have a safe trip and have fun back home in Texas."

He then gave me the address to the Djibouti Travel Bureau and told me that I would have to get my passport stamped if I expected to leave the country. I ran out of the embassy and almost got hit by a taxi. I stopped him, jumped in, and headed straight to the house. Running through the front door, I was screaming and yelling, cursing in both English and French, calling the Russians into the living room. They all came rushing in with concerned looks, thinking something was terribly wrong. I pulled the passport from my back pocket, waving it in the air. We all erupted into laughter and hollering! I gave one of the guys some money to go get food and beer to celebrate that night. And before he left, I stopped him and said, "No spirit! Vodka, okay!"

He shrugged his shoulders and said, "Vodka okay."

We drank and celebrated that night by watching those old Russian movies again.

I got my passport on Tuesday, December 15, 1998, and my flight was scheduled for December 18. Which gave me two days to get my passport stamped. So, the next morning, I grabbed a taxi and went straight to the travel bureau. The driver took me to a part of town that I had never been before. Stopping in front of some government buildings, I asked, "Where do I go now?"

Looking at me as if I was stupid, he pointed to one of the buildings, and said, "Go through those double doors, walk into the courtyard, and go up to one of the windows. Show the man your passport."

Sounds easy enough, I thought to myself. I asked the driver to wait for me, and I went in. I walked in the courtyard and waited in line at one of the windows for about thirty minutes. It felt like an eternity. It was finally my turn at the window, and I handed the clerk my passport. He opened it up and snapped at me, "Where's your arrival date, and how did you get in to this country!?"

Oh shit, he caught me off guard. I didn't expect him to ask any questions. I didn't know what to say, then the words just started flowing out of my mouth. "I came here a couple of weeks ago to visit a friend who was stationed here with the American military, and can you believe that on my first day, my suitcase got stolen with my passport in it? I've been waiting ever since for the US Embassy to issue me a new one. It finally arrived yesterday, my flight leaves Friday, and I really need to get it stamped today," I said as I was giving him the money for the stamp with an extra $100 bill for himself.

He stamped my passport and said with a smile, "Have a safe trip." I went back to the house and showed the Russians the stamp on my passport. They all shook my hand to congratulate me. Now, all I had to do was wait for Friday to roll around and make sure no one saw me for the next two days. I didn't step one foot out of that damn house.

Friday came, and I was up before the sun. My flight was scheduled to leave at ten that evening, and I couldn't keep still the entire day. I paced back and forth in the house repeatedly. I did push-ups and sit-ups and even ran in place to calm my nerves. I packed then unpacked then repacked my duffel bag to make sure I hadn't forgotten anything. I can't even count how many times I did this throughout the day. I was afraid that something was going to go wrong, or I was going to make a mistake somewhere along the line.

Finally, at 9:15 p.m., I said goodbye to the Russian guys and thanked them for their help. Even though they didn't understand a single word I was saying, I still thanked them and gave them $500 as I promised and wished them good luck. I walked out toward the main road, getting in the first taxi that was in the row and went straight to the airport. He stopped in front of the entrance to the main building of the airport, and as I was paying the driver, I noticed Djiboutian security forces x-raying the passenger's luggage before entering the main lobby. I remembered having a Bowie knife in my duffel bag, and I had to get it out before entering the building.

I didn't want to run the risk of getting stopped and questioned or even arrested so close to leaving the country. I walked to the side of the building and ducked behind some bushes near where some cars were parked. Setting my duffel bag on the ground, I pulled my bowie knife out, and tossed it underneath one of the cars. I didn't notice that a police officer had seen me walk to the side of the building and followed me. As I came back around the building, I almost bumped into him, he said in English with an Arabic accent, "I see what you are doing there!"

I replied, "I wasn't doing anything, I was just—" before I was even able to finish my sentence, he interrupted, "I saw you pissing there in those bushes!"

He was lying and didn't see what I was doing, then I asked, "What are you talking about!?"

Then he said again, "I saw you pissing in those bushes there, and you must give me $100 American dollars, or I'll report you to my sergeant. You will be arrested and taken to jail!"

I was furious. I couldn't believe what he was saying. I'm so close to getting on that plane and this asshole comes out of nowhere! I was so mad that I grabbed the officer by his arm and started pulling him toward the front entrance of the airport where his sergeant was monitoring the x-ray machine, and said angrily, "How about I take you to your sergeant and tell him that one of his officers is trying to steal money from a tourist!"

Pulling himself free from my grip, the officer gasped in fear and said, "No, no, no, it's okay, you can go. There is no problem here!"

The officer left me alone and quickly walked to his patrol car. Relieved, but still a little nervous and with my stomach in a knot, I walked toward the entrance and had my duffel bag scanned. I checked in and boarded the plane without any further problems. I sat in my seat, staring at the front door of the plane, expecting the legion's military police to walk through and arrest me at any moment. The steward closed the door, and a few minutes later, the plane slowly backed out of the terminal and onto the runway with a loud roar the plane pushed itself into the night. With a sigh of relief and a big grin, I rested back deep into my seat.

After several long delays in Paris, then in New York, I finally arrived in Austin around nine the following evening. Outside of the airport, I stopped a taxi and asked him if he could take me to San Marcos. He said that he could, but it's going to be very expensive. I then told him, "I don't care! I'll pay any price just get me to San Marcos!"

I was so exhausted and fatigued from the whole ordeal of the past couple of weeks. I immediately fell asleep. "Hey, buddy, we're in San Marcos!" the driver said, waking me up.

I pointed him the way to my family's house, and he stopped in front of it. I paid him and thanked him. The old house still looked the same, nothing had changed in the three years I was gone. The door was unlocked as always, and I walked into the kitchen and snuck into the living room where my mother and father were watching television. Not wanting to startle them, I said softly, "I'm home, Mom."

They jumped up, and the three of us hugged and cried for a long time. I whispered into her ear, "I'm never leaving the family again, Mom."

My mother went through her surgeries and doctor's visits. My father, little brother, and I were always by her side. I thank the Lord for every moment that he had given me with my mother through the good times and the bad. Her health slowly deteriorated, and in 2005, she lost both of her legs to diabetes. She returned home in a wheelchair, but her spirits were always high. She never complained about anything. She never wanted us to worry about her, but you could tell she was hiding a lot of pain. We took care of Mom for a year at home until she passed away on October 6, 2006. I dedicate this book in her loving memory.

We love and miss you, Mom.

John Paul, please watch over Mom until I get there.

Day after the farm.

Physical conditioning drills.

Resting on a road march during basic training.

My squad after the farm.

The ceremony of the Kepi blanc after the farm.

Spear fishing off the coast of Djibouti.

Our camp on the "Getting to now the men better" exercise.

Posing with a comrade after a live fire exercise.

On exercise during the tank school.

Rappelling during commando school,
we were not allowed to use gloves.

Puma helicopter landing at the start of one of
our missions during commando school.

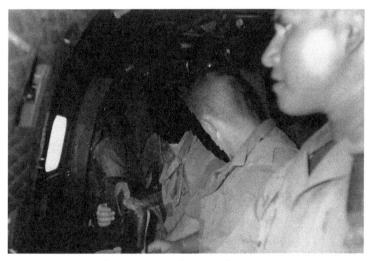

In the Puma conducting the mission.

Sneaking in some much needed rest after one of our mission.

On patrol near the Ethiopian border.

You can take the kid out of Texas but you
can never take Texas out of the kid.

The small village of We'a located outside our garrison.

The main road in the garrison.

Looking north on the main, and only, highway
in Djibouti from inside of the garrison.

The commando school badge which I still have.

Lightning Source UK Ltd.
Milton Keynes UK
UKHW051332160720
366629UK00009B/190